"Nature gave us the correct recipe."
Michael Braungart & William McDonough
(The Upcycle, North Point Press, 2013, p.221)

"The world will not evolve past its current state of crisis by using the same thinking that created the situation."
Albert Einstein
(as quoted in: *Cradle to Cradle* by Michael Braungart & William McDonough, Vintage, 2009)

AGENT C2C
Positive for People and Planet

Written by
George Hohbach & Ehrengard Hohbach
with Scott Marcano

Based on the life of Michael Braungart
Including his books
Cradle to Cradle: Remaking the Way We Make Things
and *The Upcycle*

1ˢᵗ Edition

© 2020 George Hohbach & Ehrengard Hohbach

Project Management: Scott Marcano, Diablo Productions

In anticipation of the Cradle to Cradle novels, George and Ehrengard planted 1000 trees in California in 2019 with the Environmental Charity *One Tree Planted*.
10 percent of the authors' (George & Ehrengard) revenue from each sale of the book go to the *Cradle to Cradle NGO*.

Authorization: Michael Braungart has approved Concept and Book and authorizes use of his name and copyrighted materials for inclusion and reference in Book.

Bibliographical Information of the Deutsche Nationalbibliothek
This publication is listed in the Deutsche Nationalbibliographie of the Deutsche Nationalbibliothek; detailed bibliographical information can be accessed under http: //dnb.d-nb.de

Printing and Production: BoD – Books on Demand, Norderstedt

ISBN: 978-3-7519-4280-5

AGENT C2C
Positive for People and Planet

Concept by
George Hohbach

Story by
George Hohbach & Michael Braungart

Written by
George Hohbach & Ehrengard Hohbach
with Scott Marcano

Illustrations by
Juan Romera

Illustrations of Part 2, Michael Cartoon & Title Sequence, Photos as
well as Music & Lyrics of the Song *Agent C2C* by
George Hohbach

Arrangement of the Song *Agent C2C* and Sheet Music by
Alfred Huff

English Translation of Part 2
George Hohbach with Robin Palmer, author of the acclaimed Middle
Grade book series *Yours Truly, Lucy B. Parker*

CONTENTS

PART 1
AGENT C2C
-Positive for People & Planet-

Chapter 1 – page 1

Chapter 2 – page 26

Chapter 3 – page 47

Chapter 4 – page 66

Chapter 5– page 93

Chapter 6– page 157

Chapter 7– page 211

Chapter 8– page 237

Chapter 9– page 271

Chapter 10– page 311

Song *AGENT C2C* – page 325

PART 2
About Michael Braungart &
Cradle to Cradle

– Why the Cradle to Cradle design concept makes companies, people and governments partners in striving for eco-intelligent, climate-smart solutions –
page 329

Michael Braungart – page 330

Inspirations from Michael Braungart's Life for the Story *AGENT C2C* – page 339

Acknowledgements
page 346

Appendix

Cradle to Cradle
& Albert Einstein's Findings About Symmetry
page 347

Further Reading
page 349

PART 1

AGENT C2C
-Positive for People & Planet-

CHAPTER 1

WASHINGTON, D.C., 6 AM

The morning sun had just risen above Washington, D.C. It was early spring, and the cherry trees that encircled the stately Jefferson Memorial were just starting to bloom and show off their brilliant pink blossoms. The first golden rays of dawn were falling on the White House, alighting the iconic mansion in a warm, golden glow. Indeed, the entire majestic U.S. capitol still looked quiet and serene. Inside the White House, however, there was one person who was

1

not calm, warm and cozy—the President, he was wide-awake and worried. In fact, at that very moment, he was sitting behind his desk inside the oval office, staring at his personal laptop, still dressed in his pajamas.

"This is terrible. Our entire satellite system is in jeopardy!" he barked to his CIA director, a humorless, middle-aged man whose scowling, pale face looked even grimmer than usual as he stared back at the President from a live feed on his computer.

"I've already put our best man, agent C2C, on the case, Mr. President," said the CIA director curtly. But the reassuring news did little to ease the rattled President's racing mind. The situation was enormously, catastrophically bad, and if the missing satellite wasn't found soon—it was going to get epically worse...

SOMEWHERE IN SOUTH AFRICA, 8:30 PM

At that precise moment, half-way around the world, the answer to their prayers was hurling down a mountain side on a motorcycle! Dressed in safari clothing, his handsome face masked by a wickedly cool riding helmet (one that featured a groovy green mohawk across the top), was Agent

C2C, aka "Michael" to his family, friends and fans. As he thundered down the impossibly steep hillside, Michael could see his destination dead ahead: a beautiful, grand mansion in the valley below. Inside his cool mohawked helmet, Michael's eyes scanned a flashing alert message that appeared above a large red "X" on the internal display's hologram map: "Target Located."

Michael hit the throttle—his quarry was in his crosshairs, there was no time to lose! The sprawling residence he was barreling towards stood alone and isolated in the beautiful South African countryside—whoever lived there obviously wasn't too keen on nosey neighbors. The estate looked like an opulent villa, surrounded by a huge garden and a luxurious pool with a miniature waterfall in the backyard. The place was quiet and dark right now, though, except for one room, the one Michael was zeroing in on; a large dining room behind the villa's porch. A faint glow could be seen shining through the room's white curtained windows—someone was in there.

Michael wasted no time waiting for a formal invitation to enter the magnificent estate. Instead, he cranked his motorcycle up to top speed and zoomed up a dirt embankment that buttressed the estate's perimeter. His bike was literally a blur as it sped off the end of the makeshift jump ramp and flew high into the air, just clearing the electrified fence that guarded the mansion's compound before landing with a muffled WHOMP! on the villa's spacious green lawn.

Michael skidded into a power slide to slow his momentum, then drove up a set of wide stone stairs that led up to the gardens and the main house. It was a bumpy ride going up the stairs, and in the process, he managed to knock over several fancy Grecian-style marble statues that lined the walkway—Oops! But Michael didn't care, he was completely focused on his objective. However, noise from the statues crashing loudly down the stone stairs made a terrible racket. Within seconds, alarms were sounding, and burly guards with barking dogs appeared all over the place. The guards nearest Michael drew guns and started firing at him. Michael's heart was pounding in his chest now—this situation had gotten a little more intense than he had planned!

With his element of surprise completely blown at this point, Michael opted for a more direct route to his target. He aimed the front of his motorcycle directly at the large glass door to the dining room and hit the throttle! With a huge explosion of glass and bits of wood, Michael came blasting through the door. The impact made his cool mohawk helmet fly off, revealing his mane of bushy red/blonde hair.

The helmet rolled across the floor before finally coming to a stop right in front of a couple dinning at a large table. The diners stared at Michael in shock and disbelief. The couple consisted of a husky man dressed in casual wear with a large Yin-Yang amulet hanging from his neck and a beautiful, young, Asian woman wearing an elegant evening dress. Michael skidded to a stop right in front of them.

"Good evening!" Michael said merrily. "Sorry to barge in like this on you, but I'm like totally starving, and your French onion soup over there smelled absolutely delicious. Mind if I join you?"

The husky man wearing the amulet wasn't amused by his joke. He snatched a large steak knife off the table and tried to plunge it into Michael's chest. Michael dodged the blow and counterattacked with a fist punch and a round house kick to the beefy man's jaw. Foot met chin with a loud whack! The burly man flew backwards and tumbled to the floor half-way across the room—knocked out cold. Michael calmly strolled over to him and ripped off the Yin-Yang amulet off his neck. He put the medallion into a pocket of his pants.

Michael glanced at the gorgeous woman at the table.

Her pretty brown eyes were filled with fear, but Michael gave her a short, sweet, smile.

"Don't worry, my dear," he said reassuringly to the pretty woman still seated at the table. "I'm obviously not here to hurt anyone, especially someone as pretty as you." In spite of her fear, the young woman couldn't help blushing a little. Michael grabbed an open bottle of champagne off the table and refilled her glass.

"Enjoy!" he said with a chuckle. He was about to pour himself a glass, too, but just then, screaming guards waving big guns, accompanied by their wild, vicious dogs, came rushing into the dining room. Michael sighed.

"Maybe some other time," Michael said to the lovely young woman.

He winked at her, took a quick swig of champagne straight from the bottle and jumped back on his motorcycle. Quickly, he hit the throttle and sped away, blasting right through a window. The guards ran up to the broken window, firing their guns in futility as Agent C2C rocketed across the back lawn and disappeared into the night.

The elegant party on the 10th floor of the large, modern high-rise was in full swing. One floor above, Michael, aka Agent C2C, crept slowly out of an air vent. He carefully lowered himself out of the air duct and did a small, noiseless jump down onto the floor of the spacious office below. His landing wasn't as smooth as he had planned, however, as his leg bumped against a table, knocking a decorative porcelain vase over. Just in time, Michael's hands hot out, and he caught the precious pot just before it crashed on the floor. Michael took a deep breath and placed the delicate vase back on the table. He shook his head—wow, that was close!

Michael quickly surveyed his surroundings. On the wall across from him, he spotted a painting depicting the eight trigrams chart of I Ching. In the center of the chart was a Yin-Yang symbol. A look of revelation swept across Michael's face. He tip-toed over to the painting, took out his Yin-Yang amulet and placed it directly on the painting's identical symbol. Instantly, the amulet clicked into unseen grooves, and then, a secret door slid open along the wall!

Without hesitation, Michael rushed through the secret entrance. On the other side, he found himself standing in what looked like another, identical office. This office was like the original except for a few important details. For one, it was windowless, and two, all the computers and other electronic equipment was super high-end. Whatever operation went on in here, it was obviously very sophisticated and without a doubt—totally illegal.

Michael started quickly searching the hidden room. For a few moments, his search was fruitless. Then, inside the drawers of the expensive mahogany desk, he suddenly found what he was looking for: pictures of a huge yacht bearing the name *JUPITER*. On top of the yacht, there were a large satellite disk and multiple state-of-the-art naval antennas. Michael whipped out his smart phone and snapped off a few pictures of the yacht. Then, he quietly put everything back in place and slinked soundlessly out of the hidden office.

Michael placed a small black disc on the floor in the main office and went out into the dark hallway. There, he took off his black "cat-burglar" gear and threw it into a trash can. Underneath, he wore an expensive tuxedo. He straightened his bow tie and made a few other small adjustments to his attire before heading down the stairs to enter the loud party on the floor below.

Inside the party room, guests were dancing, dining

and enjoying drinks which countless waiters served up to them at a snap of their fingers. Michael mingled casually with the crowd for a few moments as he made his way towards an exit on the far side of the room. Quickly, he grabbed a glass of champagne off a tray along the way and guzzled it down.

He was almost at the exit when a beautiful young Asian woman, dressed in a silver cocktail dress, sitting at the bar, turned around and smiled at him.

"You're leaving again already?" she said with a bemused smile on her face.

Michael instantly recognized her: it was the very attractive girl he had flirted with when he busted into the secluded mansion a few nights ago in South Africa. Michael knew her name by now. He'd learned it during his debriefing from his previous mission. She wasn't just another pretty face—she was a professional agent just like him.

"Agent Lee," Michael said with a smirk, "what a lovely coincidence."

"Hardly, Agent C2C. I just hope, you were a bit more subtle than last time."

"Just a tad."

Suddenly, an ear-splitting boom rang out as a huge explosion shook the entire building. It was the small disc-shaped bomb Michael had left upstairs. As chaos descended across the room, sirens started to wail, and armed guards appeared all over the place.

"Damn," Michael said with a shrug as he brushed bits of fallen plaster off his shoulder, "that was supposed to go off *after* I made my exit. I guess, I should have given myself some extra time on the countdown to allow for running into you wearing such a stunning dress."

Agent Lee just shook her head and laughed at him. "Always gotta make a scene, don't you? I just can't take you anywhere."

They looked around and saw that the armed guards had begun to seal off all the exits. One of them spotted Michael and narrowed his eyes on him.

"Uh-oh, I think I've been spotted," Michael said.

"Well, that mangy red/blonde mop-top is kinda hard to miss," quipped Agent Lee.

Michael frowned at her, then scowled even harder as he watched the guard get the attention of other guards and gesture emphatically at them. The men started rushing towards them, aiming their guns!

"Guess, we're escaping through the kitchen this time!" said Agent Lee as she slid off her bar stool and removed a small round object from her purse.

"Sounds delicious! Let's move!"

Agent Lee hurled the round object down on the ground just as the guards were almost upon them. The smoke grenade exploded on contact, sending up a small cloud of dense white smoke. The stunned guards were instantly blinded. In the momentary confusion, Michael and Agent Lee dashed quickly into the kitchen as the pack of disoriented, coughing guards stumbled along in pursuit.

NORWEGIAN SEA, 3 AM

A bright full moon hung low in the starry sky over the shimmering sea. Presently, two dark objects floated through the cold air serenely into view, gliding slowly down out of the heavens; a pair of parachutes…

Michael and Agent Lee steered their chutes onto the empty top deck of a large, luxury yacht that was moored just below them. They landed without a sound and unharnessed themselves from their parachutes. They immediately donned night vision googles and rushed through an open hatch that led to the inside of the ship.

A few moments later, they suddenly burst into the control room and instantly dispatched several shocked guards and crew persons with a series of lightening quick marital arts moves. Once the control room was secure, they turned their attention to a large display screen at the front of the room. It depicted the flight paths of countless satellites—a countdown showed 18 seconds left on the clock. Agent Lee turned a little pale.

"We got 15 seconds to disable the computer or all our satellites will stop working!" she cried.

"We better hurry up then!" Michael said as he opened a small door on a central computer control panel.

Michael peered inside and saw a tangled mess of wires. Some were red, others orange, blue, green, yellow, even purple—it looked like a rainbow-colored blob of spaghetti! Michael gulped.

"If we disconnect the wrong one, the shutdown will commence immediately," Agent Lee yelled.

"Don't be so optimistic." Michael took out a pair of pliers from his pocket and began desperately hunting for the right ones to clip.

"Seven seconds! Quick, Michael!" Agent Lee announced.

Franticly, Michael continued his search. It could be any of them! The veins on his neck were bulging from the stress.

"Three seconds!"

In that instant, Michael saw two distinct wires that stood out in the mass of twisted cables; one was *white,* the other *black.* Right away, a recollection of the Yin-Yang symbol flashed through his mind. Instinctively, he acted. The countdown went to 2, then 1, then… it stopped. Agent Lee was gasping. She couldn't believe that the countdown had come to a halt. Quickly, she looked at Michael who was holding the ends of the two clipped wires.

"You cut both wires?!" she exclaimed, pointing at the black and white cables.

"Yin and Yang," Michael replied with a smile.

A grin spread across Agent Lee's pretty face. "Nice work, Agent C2C."

"Right back at you, Agent Lee."

Their eyes met and lingered on each other for a moment—now, with the tension gone, they could allow their feelings of mutual attraction to flow more freely.

"Well, since the world is safe again, maybe we should blow this taco stand and find some cool place to just kick back and chill," offered Michael hopefully.

"Totally agree," Agent Lee beamed. "I know just the place…"

With a proud tone in his voice, the very relieved U.S. President briefed his equally very relieved counterpart, the Chinese Premier, via his laptop. Once all the details of the raid on the South African villa, the Singapore high-rise and the fancy yacht had been shared, the two men congratulated themselves for a job well done saving the world. Both acknowledged, however, that the real heroes of the operation were their respective countries' incredible super agents: C2C and Lee.

"Those two bad-asses really deserve a medal!" said the Chinese Premier. "I'd love to tell them both personally what an incredible job they both did—if only we could find them. They disappeared right after the raid on the yacht."

"Don't worry," replied the American President. "Through our advanced tracking technology, we were just able to locate agents C2C and Lee. They're in the Bahamas. We have a satellite connection and can talk to them now."

"Excellent!" said the smiling Chinese Premier.

Agent C2C and Agent Lee kissed passionately as they got hot and heavy on the king-sized bed in their luxurious bungalow suite. Overcome with pent up emotion, they literally began to tear apart and rip off each other's clothes!

Unnoticed by them, however, a miniature, nano-sized electronic bug on top of their TV suddenly came to life. It quickly established a connection to a top-secret spy satellite, which, in turn, relayed data back to the White House and Beijing. Caught up in the moment, neither C2C nor Lee noticed their TV suddenly turn on as it began streaming live two-way video back to the President and the Chinese Premier...

Back in their respective offices, the two world leaders stared in shock and embarrassment as images of their two top agents making out appeared on their monitors.

"Wow, awkward," said the shocked U.S. President.

"Agent, Lee!" the Chinese Premier shouted angrily.

This got Michael and Lee's attention. They looked around, confused for a moment, before noticing the scowling face of the Chinese Premier right next to the President's on a split screen on the suite's large screen TV. Lee's face

16

turned bright red.

"Oh! Hi there, sir! What a pleasant surprise!" she blurted out quickly in Chinese as she tried to cover up her partially naked body with a tiny throw pillow. The Premier didn't look amused.

Lee bit her lip and whispered into Michael's ear: "I did not see that coming when we saved the world's satellite system."

"Your clothes!" said the American President pointing at the ripped garments lying on the floor and dangling off their bodies.

"Oh, don't worry, gentlemen," Michael replied with a friendly smile, "we are modern, international agents. All our equipment, including our clothes, is fully recyclable."

The President and the Premier didn't really know how to respond to that. Michael decided it might be a good idea to make things a lot less uncomfortable for everyone. So, he reached over to the electronic bug, swatted it off the TV and then crushed it with his foot. The satellite feed went dead. The TV screen turned black. Michael shock his head and sighed.

"Technology really can be your best friend or worst enemy these days," he said.

Lee giggled. "So true."

17

"Where were we again, Agent Lee?"

"We were working on deepening the relationship between our countries and also getting our clothes ready for composting!"

"Right, right." Michael leaned in close to Agent Lee. "Let's get back to work then, shall we?"

They began kissing heavily again and ripping off their remaining clothes. They threw their ripped garments out an open window of the bungalow. On the other side of the window, their clothes fell to the ground and piled up in a lush garden below. Instantly, the fabric of the ripped clothes began to disintegrate and compost. Within seconds, it had turned into nutrient rich soil—

Out of which a beautiful flower grew...

... Then, the image of the budding flower faded slowly to black as text appeared on the screen: "The End?"

Lights came on as the promotional film ended. It was 10 AM inside the large, packed convention hall of the *International Business Leaders Conference* in Washington, D.C. The crowd, that had just watched the thrilling spy-themed environmentally conscious short, applauded enthusiastically. More words now appeared on the large screen in the background of the stage:

POSITIVE FOR PEOPLE & PLANET

FULL CYCLES ONLY

The words faded away, except for the three letters "C2C" which remained on the screen and shone in bright yellow letters. A spotlight hit the stage as the young, world-renowned chemistry professor and co-founder of the Cradle to Cradle design concept, Michael Braungart, strode confidently onto the podium. His arrival was greeted with even louder applause. Michael smiled back warmly towards the audience which consisted of international business VIPs, prominent leaders of NGOs, political leaders from around the world as well as young environmental activists. Judging by the enthusiastic response, it was clear, everyone in attendance very much enjoyed the fact that Michael had starred in the Cradle to Cradle promotion clip playing himself as the super-smart secret agent with a twinkle in his eye.

"It's true, that's what I actually do for a living!" Michael joked as he scratched his curly, slightly disorganized hair. "Being a millennial chemistry professor is just a side hobby that I use as a cover for my espionage work." The audience roared with laughter. "Seriously, though," Michael continued, "with Cradle to Cradle, or in short, *the C2C Concept*, there is no waste any longer in this world, because all the products that utilize Cradle to Cradle principals are designed in such a way that their materials and substances can be fully reused perpetually. Just like in nature, C2C works with the concept of the nutrient cycle. All substances are nutrients, either as healthy ones in the biosphere, or if they are poisonous but valuable, in the closed technosphere."

A large, green human footprint appeared on the screen behind Michael, and he continued, "That way, we can grow our ecological human footprint, because all we do, based on the C2C concept, will be beneficial to both planet and people. C2C aims for achieving improvements for all, man and environment—including our climate, of course. Countless companies and government organizations around the world are implementing the C2C scheme—and you and your companies, organizations and authorities can be part of this positive revolution as well."

A quick montage of disgusting images of human waste, in all its destructive forms, now appeared on the screen behind Michael. A depressed murmur went through the room. The last image depicted garbage piled up in the ocean and next to it, a dead sea bird. The bird's belly had been cut open to reveal that its stomach was full of plastic. This last image made the audience squirm.

"I know, pretty sad and gross, right?" Michael said, shaking his head. "But here's the good news, folks: If you wanna actively start cleaning the ocean right now, at this convention in Washington, D.C. and become a waste management activist, all you have to do is to eat as many of the polluted oysters as possible from the lovely buffet we'll serve soon. Oysters are full of small, colorful plastic particles, because oysters filter the ocean's water."

Again, a somewhat depressed laughter filled the room.

Michael paused for a moment, then continued: "Traditionally, we talk about zero waste, zero emissions. But this makes absolutely no sense. All living creatures produce something, especially waste, or normally, as I should say, valuable nutrients for their environment. If you want to produce zero emissions, that's not even possible when you're dead. You must not exist if you want to be Mr. and Mrs. 'Zero Emissions'. So, since zero emissions makes no sense, you have to make sure that what you produce is designed to be positive for all living things from the start.

Then, what you do is good for both planet and people. That is how nature works, and we are part of nature. Unfortunately, *sustainability* is a very overused, misunderstood concept. People think of *sustainability* as a goal that solves everything, but more often than not, the concept is misused and applied to the wrong things, like, for example, the production of toxic waste. The problem with trying to make everything *sustainable* is that being sustainable doesn't mean you're really solving a problem. It just means, you're trying to be *less bad*—which in the long run will destroy everything even more thoroughly. That is the dark truth of sustainability. It means '*somehow getting along, just being able to cope with something*'. No fun, no joy, but lots of guilty feelings about everything. What a sad word."

Michael walked right up to the front of the stage as the spotlight followed him. In the middle of the first row sat Sydney Munger, the real-life U.S. President. As he approached the most powerful man in the world, Michael felt the muscles on the back of his neck tighten. He was very nervous. He saw the sharp eyes of the Secret Service agents, who guarded the President, zero in on him.

Thoughts flashed through his head, "*Should I really do this? Will the President play along with my joke?*" But there was no time to really think about it, so he decided to just go for it!

"If I asked you, Mr. President," Michael said, using a smile to cover up his growing nervousness, "'how is your relationship with your wife?', and if you replied, 'It's sustainable', then all I could say is: 'I'm so sorry for you and especially for your wife.'"

Laughter instantly filled the auditorium. President Munger laughed, too. Michael quietly let out a sigh of relief. *"Thank God,"* Michael thought to himself, *"the man's got a good sense of humour!"*

But suddenly, President Munger spoke up, loud enough for everyone to hear. "Speaking of private lives, how's yours going as the world's latest smart super-agent, Professor Braungart?!"

Laughs shot through the room. That kind of reaction by the leader of the free world, Michael was not expecting. Swallowing down yet another rush of nervousness, Michael jumped into the humorous spirit of the moment and replied loudly:

"Wow. The U.S. President has seriously just asked me, how my private life as a brilliant super-agent is? You're sure, you really wanna know how amazing it is?" Michael smiled at President Munger, then looked at the audience with a twinkle in his eye. "If I tell you that, I'm afraid all of your wives will run out on you!"

More howls of laughter echoed through the auditorium.

"It's true... and I'll tell you this, too: Let us celebrate abundance, like nature does, by using materials that are both positive and safe for humans and the environment, and that can continually be recycled without losing their quality in a revolutionary, circular economy."

Michael took out a T-shirt from his jacket pocket. He held it up high, so that everybody could see it.

"Then you can, like this T-shirt here, throw used goods away into nature, as the materials will become nutrients and quality soil."

With that, Michael tossed the T-shirt onto the other side of the stage. Instantly, a spotlight hit it. As if by magic, the T-shirt instantly dissolved and was replaced by a beautiful, blossoming cherry tree! The audience "oohed" and "ahhed".

"Nature gave us the correct recipe," Michael continued, "with its natural cycle that doesn't try to eliminate waste, but rather turns it into positive nutrients—like this gorgeous cherry tree. This tree will flourish and produce an overabundance of nourishing fruits, its leaves and countless pedals will become rich soil, and it will absorb

CO_2 while releasing valuable oxygen as its positive emission. That is how nature works. If we all implement nature's scheme of this positive nutrient cycle, not only in the natural realm, but in our technosphere as well, then we all, seven, eight or even 20 billion people can have fun on this planet."

A large picture of Albert Einstein appeared on the screen in the background. "Einstein, who mathematically showed us, using the simple concept of symmetry, that everything in the universe—and, therefore, in nature—is interconnected, put it that way: *'The world will not evolve past its current state of crisis by using the same thinking that created the situation.'* Let us follow Einstein's smart advice. Let's behave like nature shows us. Let's go for FULL CYCLES ONLY!"

With these words, the picture of planet earth appeared on the screen along with a large revolving circle that surrounded humanity's amazing home in the infinite and miraculous universe. A wave of applause vibrated through the giant convention hall as the participants in the conference rose to their feet and cheered.

CHAPTER 2

SECRET U.S. MILITARY LAB

The military jeep made its way methodically up a steep, winding, desert road. It was headed for a range of towering, jagged mountains that rose up sharply off the desert plane like stone daggers in the distance. The range was known as the Organ Mountains, and locals sometimes jokingly referred to it as "the goblin's teeth" because of the mountains somewhat ominous appearance. The imposing ridges bordered the desolate region in southern New Mexico that was sandwiched between the bustling small town of Las Cruces and the U.S. Army Missile Test Range in White Sands. Because of its remoteness, the area was home to several top-secret military testing and research facilities. The jeep was headed for one of the most sensitive and secret stations here—one that the army had actually carved deep into the side of a mountain.

The facility's entrance was surrounded by a huge, electrified fence crowned with concertina wire strewn across the top. Surveillance cameras, some hidden inside fake rocks and cacti, were everywhere, surveying anyone who approached within several miles of the restricted area. Behind the heavily guarded front gate, the entrance to the underground base was clearly visible; a giant steel door built right into the side of the sheer mountain.

Silent alarms alerted the men guarding the facility that the jeep was approaching. A very serious looking, heavily armed soldier accompanied by a barking dog came out of a booth next to the front gate. He signaled for the approaching jeep to halt. The car came to a stop in front of him. A grizzled, stern-looking, middle aged man dressed in a colonel's uniform sat behind the steering wheel. Without looking at the soldier, he handed the man his ID.

"Good morning, Colonel," said the surprised guard

as he looked over the ID. Silently, the Colonel placed his right index finger on a portable scanner that the soldier held in his hand. Instantly, the device gave its findings: "ID confirmed. Cleared for Entry."

"Welcome to the lab, sir!" The soldier signaled to a colleague inside the booth. A section of the electrified fence slid aside, and a steel barricade bar lifted up, allowing the Colonel to drive onto the premises. The huge, imposing metal doors swung open up on the side of the mountain, revealing a large tunnel leading deep inside the earth. The jeep cruised along the road and entered the mountain. Once it headed in, the steel doors immediately swung shut behind it with a loud metallic clang that echoed away through the empty desert...

Ten minutes later, the Colonel, accompanied by two nervous soldiers, walked down a dimly lit corridor.

"We were not informed of your visit, sir," said one of the antsy soldiers.

"That's how it's supposed to be," growled the Colonel. "That's why it's called an *unannounced inspection*, idiot! Do you have a problem with that?"

The soldiers instantly shook their heads. "No, sir. I'm sure you'll find everything in perfect order, sir!"

"I better," said the Colonel gruffly, "or somebody's ass, probably yours, is gonna be in a sling. You hear me!?" The soldiers nodded emphatically and quietly gulped.

Moments later, the three men arrived at an ultra-secure steel door that was protected by numerous locks. A stencil on the front read "storage", and a bio-hazard warning symbol was displayed prominently beneath it. The lead soldier punched a secret code into a keypad and positioned his right eye in front of a retinal scanner. Silently, a red laser beam passed over his retina. A green light on the keypad went on, then, multiple locks disengaged, and the door swung open.

The Colonel and the two nervous soldiers entered a sparse storage room. The two soldiers looked very apprehensive to even be in here. Numerous bottles and vials were arrayed along long shelves across the space. Each one was marked with an identification number on it. The Colonel looked around with a critical eye.

"Don't tell me this room has no surveillance cameras in it," he barked at his guides.

"It does, sir," said the lead soldier. He pointed up at a lone camera that hung from the ceiling in the corner of the room. "That one right up there."

"Just one?" asked the Colonel sceptically.

"Uhhh… Yes, sir," said the anxious soldier.

The Colonel shook his head. "Where's the inventory for all these items?"

"Right here, sir!" said the second soldier. He turned and gestured to an iPad that was hanging on a hook near the door. The Colonel snapped his fingers twice, indicating, "Give it to me!" The lead soldier took the iPad off the hook and opened a file marked "inventory". He handed it to the Colonel who browsed through the document on the screen rapidly, checking off names of items and matching them with their code numbers.

"This inventory is complete and up to date?" muttered the Colonel.

"Yes, sir. We double check it daily."

"That so? Well then, show me item #292. Pronto!" the Colonel bellowed as he touched the underscored number 292 on the screen.

In the distance, a red light instantly began flashing at the front of one of the shelves. The two men scrambled quickly to find the requested object next to the light signal.

"Here it is, sir!" one of them said. Very carefully, he removed the item from its holding case on the shelf and brought it over to the Colonel. It was a vial filled with a purple liquid. The glass vial was tagged with numerous symbols indicating that whatever was inside was an extremely hazardous substance. The Colonel didn't seem too concerned about this as he looked over the vial for a moment, holding it rather casually in his hands as he sloshed the strange purple liquid back and forth.

"Hmmm… So beautiful and, yet—so deadly, like a ninja disguised as a geisha," said the Colonel with a smirk.

The two soldiers nodded and smirked as well, but eyed the vial warily, their minds racing with thoughts of what would happen if the Colonel accidentally dropped it on the floor.

"That doesn't look right," the Colonel said suddenly.

"What doesn't, sir?" asked the lead soldier.

"The camera, dummy, up there." The Colonel pointed up at the surveillance camera on the ceiling. "The angle is off. It looks like it doesn't cover the whole room." The soldiers peered at it, trying to decide. "Maybe, sir."

"No *maybes* about it. It's definitely off. Here, I'll show you. Stand over there in the far corner."

The two soldiers walked over to the corner of the room and looked up at the surveillance camera; it was obvious from this vantage point, that the lens wasn't pointing at them. The Colonel tucked the vial of deadly liquid into his front pocket and strolled over to them.

"See, we're off screen here. If intruders snuck in, they could stand right in this spot and the security would never see them—they could do anything they liked, and no one would ever know."

"That's true, sir," said the lead soldier, "but they would have to find a way to get in here first—it's a pretty small hole in our game to exploit."

"That's all, a true professional needs," replied the Colonel as he suddenly whipped a small pistol affixed with a silencer from his pocket. Before the two stunned men could react, he shot them both in the head! The two men instantly collapsed to the floor. Dead. The Colonel looked down at them and shook his head.

"See, what I'm talking about?" The Colonel took out a small, metal box from his pocket and opened it. Inside was a foam casing with an empty vial shaped space. He placed the vial of deadly fluid in the box, carefully sealed it and tucked it (along with the pistol) back in his pocket. Then, he strolled calmly out the room, calling out loudly behind him so that whoever was monitoring the room could hear:

"You two wait right there, don't move until I come back. I need to talk to your superior officer about this!"

A few minutes later, the security guards opened the exterior gate and saluted as the stone-faced Colonel drove past them and sped off quickly. After he had gotten a safe distance from the secret facility, the Colonel smiled to himself. He reached up and took a firm grasp of the skin on the edge of his face. He gave it a hard tug and ripped off a custom-made latex mask that had been covering his real face! He also pulled off a latex coating from his index finger that he had used to fool the guard's fingerprint ID scanner.

Beneath the disguise of the slightly grizzled army Colonel was a handsome, intense looking man in his late forties. Those in the know would instantly recognize him as international terrorist, Alex Torex—one of the most wanted men in the world!

Torex took the metal box with the vial of mysterious liquid inside out of his pocket and tossed it on the seat next to him. He rubbed the top of the metal box lovingly—as if it were made of pure gold. Then, he let out a chilling, high-pitched laugh that sounded like the unsettling noise a hyena makes after a fresh kill.

Torex punched a button on his car's audio system, and his favourite hip-hop song came blasting out of the speakers. Alex bobbed his head to the infectious beat and stomped the gas pedal. The car roared off into the desert, heading for a destination unknown…

WASHINGTON, D.C.

Michael exited the entrance of the D.C. Convention Center, walking briskly beneath a large digital screen that read:

THE INTERNATIONAL FORUM
ON ENVIRONMENTAL ECONOMIC
DEVELOPMENT

Michael was in a big hurry, but he took the time to quickly sign a few autographs for some fans hanging around the entrance before hustling over to the curb, where an orange Tesla Model S was waiting for him. Michael hopped in, and the car instantly sped off. In the backseat, next to Michael, was his lovely and capable young assistant, Chantal. His long-time driver, Max, glanced over his shoulder at him.

"Hi, boss," said Max with a friendly smile.

"Hiya, Max," Michael replied warmly.

Chantal, however, wasn't in a happy mood. "Finally, you're here!" Chantal said, nervously. "We'll be lucky to make it to the airport on time."

"Isn't that what we do?" Michael replied with a bemused smile on his lips.

"Maybe planes should generally just start late, as a rule, like baseball games," Chantal wondered aloud. She glanced at Michael with a look of deep admiration in her eyes. "By the way, *you* were amazing in there!"

Chantal opened up her laptop and turned the screen so Michael could see it. She quickly navigated to a video posted on GSNC-TV (the Global Sphere News Channel TV) of the speech Michael had just given where he joked around with the President and explained the concept of C2C. The video had already gone completely viral, receiving millions of views.

"Your joke exchange with the President has gone viral, congratulations."

"Excellent!" Michael said with a fist pump.

Chantal continued: "Because of that, the C2C Promo clip with you as 'Agent C2C' went viral, too. But that's not all, several magazines are now calling you '*Sexiest Man Alive!*'"

"You're joking, right?" said Michael with a laugh, but Chantal shook her head.

"Nope, they really are. My phone is totally blowing

up. All the major U.S. networks wanna do interviews with you. Drug companies are calling to see if you can create a new virility miracle pill for men over 50, and major publishing companies have emailed me that they offer you 30 million in advance if you write a book like *The Guide to a smart super agent's Sex Life by Prof. Braungart*. I, I mean—" Michael cut her off, "That's hilarious! Really, I'm flattered and all, but come on! My ass is as flat as the Australian outback, but all of a sudden, I'm the '*Sexiest Man Alive*'. Think about it, I don't even comb my hair, nor do I take cold showers in the morning." Michael sighed happily. "Well, I guess, it just proves: There is no such thing as bad press as long as it is positive."

Chantal nodded in agreement. "I bet you made the 11 o' clock news." She flipped on the TV in the backrest of the passenger seat.

GSNC-TV came on. A middle-aged anchor with a salt and pepper hair, named Ralf Richard Mann, was on. He was in the middle of a report. A graphic behind him showed a picture of the infamous Asian dictator Jimbo Jam, a pudgy-looking man in his mid-thirties, surrounded by nuclear missiles. A headline on the top of the graphic screamed:

JIMBO JAM FLEXES HIS NUCLEAR
MUSCLES!

"Apparently, this time it is serious," said Ralf, grimly. "According to Pentagon officials, North Legeria dictator Jimbo Jam allegedly obtained new nuclear missiles."

"Who cares!" scoffed Chantal. She patted Michael's leg. "I bet you're next."

On the TV screen, a new picture appeared. It was an official photo of the missing Colonel who had been impersonated by the terrorist Torex! Michael looked concerned, but Chantal merely let out a loud "ugh!"

"When are they going to get to the real news," she demanded as Ralf continued:

"According to military officials, Army Colonel, Harrison Port, has gone missing. Our sources indicate that this case might be linked to an incident at a highly classified U.S. military research lab earlier today, where, as sources say, a break-in occurred. We reached out to the Pentagon for comment but were told the military had no further statements at this time. We'll keep you posted on this troubling incident as we gather more information."

"Yeah, yeah, blah-blah-blah!" said Chantal impatiently.

Just then, a picture of Michael Braungart appeared on screen with the headline:

SEXIEST MAN ALIVE!

Chantal let out a triumphant yell. "Yes! I knew they'd report about you first!"

On the TV screen, Ralf gestured to Michael's picture behind him. "If you don't already know him, that's a picture of 'Agent C2C'—aka Michael Braungart, co-founder of the Cradle to Cradle concept, the man everyone is talking about! Many people, including leading experts on Climate Change and the economy, think he has initiated the next industrial revolution together with his American business partner, renowned architect William McDonough. And now, on top of saving the planet, this unassuming millennial-aged chemist has been voted the 'Sexiest Man Alive'. All I can say, as a fellow man of a certain mature age, is: Good for you, Michael! And by the way, I'm totally jealous!"

Chantal flipped off the TV. Beaming with joy, she pointed excitedly at Michael. "See! I told you! You're the man, everyone is talking about!"

Michael looked somewhat embarrassed. "I'm so glad, you're giving the word *modesty* a whole new meaning."

Just then, Chantal's laptop let out a "ping!" sound. A new email had landed in her inbox. The subject line read: "Great!" Chantal glanced at the sender, her eyes got a little bigger when she saw who it was from.

"Peggy Munger just sent you an email. Is that—"

"Yes, it's President Munger's daughter," replied Michael casually as he took Chantal's laptop from her and read the email out loud:

Hi, Michael,
I just watched your latest talk and joke with dad.
G8! LOL!
Hope 2 see U soon, Agent C2C!
Best,
Peggy

Chantal looked confused. "*Hope to see you soon*?! Is there something going on between you and the President's daughter?" she asked suspiciously.

"Yes," said Michael with a deadpan expression on his face, "it's called an email exchange."

BANGKOK, THAILAND

At that moment, halfway across the world, Peggy Munger, the President's extremely bright but rebellious, eighteen-year-old daughter sat behind a desk in a luxurious hotel room in Thailand's buzzling capital. Strangely, even though, she was in one of the ritziest hotels in the world, she was wearing a dark, rugged, hiking outfit.

Peggy's notebook sat open in front of her. She was scrolling through her emails and glanced at the email reply she just received from Michael. It displayed a smiley face emoji, underneath it read: *"Best wishes, Michael."* With a smile, Peggy closed her laptop. She tucked it into a large backpack. Then, she paused for a moment and surveyed the suite, making sure she hadn't forgotten anything. Satisfied that she had everything covered, Peggy put on the backpack and quietly slipped out the door.

As Peggy exited her room, she encountered two Secret Service agents dressed in suits, wearing sunglasses, sprawled out in chairs on either side of the door. They were fast asleep and snoring loudly. One of them had a half-finished Sudoku puzzle lying across his lap. On a small table beside them, were two empty bottles of vitamin drinks.

Peggy considered the snoring agents for a moment with a satisfied smirk across her face. Then, she bent down to them and whispered:

"Told you, those vitamin drinks would kill your jetlag. Sleep tight, kids!"

Peggy plucked the sunglasses off one of the agents' faces and put them on. She pulled up the hood of her jacket over her head and sauntered over to the elevator.

Once she reached the hotel lobby, Peggy dashed around a column to avoid being seen by other Secret Service agents posted around the room. She waited there for a few moments until a large group of guests walked by, heading for the exit. When they came close enough, Peggy quickly slithered out from behind the column and walked beside the group, using them as a screen to block the agents from seeing her. The subterfuge worked to perfection, and she slipped right out the front doors of the hotel without anyone noticing.

When she was safely outside, Peggy immediately jumped into a waiting cab. She tossed her backpack onto the backseat as the driver, an overly excited young man, whipped his head around and greeted her with a toothy grin.

"Where to, miss?" he asked in accented English.

"You wanna find a party, yo?! Get your game on, yo?! Well, you got in the right cab, miss, I know all the best clubs in town, yo!"

"No, thanks, yo," Peggy said, "I just need to get here."

She handed him a print-out of a map she had downloaded from Google. The map showed a remote region far away from the city with a particular location circled in red. The driver looked at the map and almost burst out laughing.

"Sorry, I can't take you there, miss. I'm just a city cab, yo. That's like on the other side of freaking Cambodia!"

Peggy responded by handing the man an envelope. The driver opened it and peered inside; it was filled with dollars. Lots and lots of dollars—all of them had Ben Franklin's face printed on them. The driver's eyes bugged out. He mouthed the equivalent of "holy crap" in Thai and immediately fired up his cab.

"Let me know if you want me to stop for food along the way."

"No stops—just go. Now!" Peggy demanded.

The driver stomped on the gas pedal, and they peeled out.

The cab drove all night long, passing through the tangled, sprawling metropolis, then through the surrounding countryside, until it reached the jungle rainforest. There it drove along a rut-filled dirt road before it finally stopped at the head of a little-used hiking trail.

It was dawn now. They were very deep in the forest. Meanwhile, the first rays of sunlight were starting to illuminate the dense foliage. All around, the hum of insects and the melodic tweets and songs of various tropical birds filled the air. Peggy climbed out of the cab with her backpack and stretched her stiff legs. She scanned the area and noticed a young Asian man in his twenties, leaning up inconspicuously against a tree at the trailhead. Like her, the Asian man was wearing dark hiking gear and sunglasses.

He looked at Peggy and strolled over to her. Without saying a word, Peggy handed him an envelope filled with bills. He nodded.

Peggy turned back to the cab driver. "This never happened. You never saw me."

"Saw who, yo?" the cab driver said with a mischievous smile. He hit the gas and drove off quickly.

Peggy waited a moment or two for the cab to disappear down the rutty dirt road, then she turned back to the silent Asian man. She gestured for him to lead the way.

The two hikers then set off, marching up a winding path, heading deeper into the lush rainforest. As they walked along, the guide began to whistle a tune over and over again. Peggy wasn't sure what the song was, but it sounded a lot like an Asian version of *99 Bottles of Beer on The Wall.* At first, Peggy didn't mind the serenade too much, but after a while the monotonous tune got pretty annoying. Finally, she decided that she couldn't take it anymore. She turned to her guide.

"I'm sorry, I don't mean to be rude or anything, but could you just chill and not whistle that anymore, or at least change the tune? That cringy song is really starting to bug the living crap out of me."

Rather than stopping, the guide completely ignored her request and continued chirping out his irritating, repetitive melody. Peggy shook her head and muttered "thanks" under her breath. Onward they went.

They hiked for several more hours, going higher and higher along the circuitous trail that led up a steep mountainside. Passing by big, hissing snakes, jumping spiders and other grunting and roaring hungry wildlife, sent cold shivers down Peggy's spine. Luckily, humans were not on the predators' menu list, plus the guide had a pistol with him—just in case one of the animals wanted to treat them as breakfast.

Finally, as Peggy's nerves had almost reached their breaking point from the monotonous song, they arrived at the peak. Mercifully, the guide finally stopped whistling.

Ahead of them, Peggy could see an endless expanse of mountainous terrain separated from them by a tall barbed wire fence that ran along the entire ridge. There was a large sign attached to it. Words written in Thai indicated this was a national border of some kind and warned that the barrier shouldn't be crossed. The guide gestured towards a small hole that had been cut in the barbed wire fence. Beyond the breech was a trail that lead down the mountain and off into the jungle. Peggy looked at the guide.

"So, this is where the fun part starts, right?" The silent guide just stared at her.

"Right," Peggy said to herself. She reached into her backpack and pulled out a big machete. "Thanks for all your help, bro. It's been real."

Peggy walked over to the fence and carefully climbed through the small hole. She headed off alone, hacking away at the overgrowth as she went down the trail. More fear started to bubble up inside of her. She wondered if she should have asked the guide for his pistol… But then again, carrying a weapon could get her killed on this side of the fence. Sometimes, the options were just too great.

The silent guide watched her go. "Good luck," he said quietly to himself, "you'll need it..." He then turned and started back down the mountain, whistling his annoying tune again as he disappeared back into the rainforest.

CHAPTER 3

WASHINGTON, D.C.

Inside the oval office, the worried U.S. President watched footage from the heist at the U.S. military laboratory in New Mexico. As he viewed the disturbing images of the murdered soldiers' bodies being carted out of the storage room, he glanced down and stared at a picture of his wife, Susan, and daughter, Peggy, sitting on his desk—it was an instinctive comforting habit he did whenever he was stressed.

His top national security advisor, Robert Jordan, the head of the CIA, and other several high-ranking military representatives were present, waiting for President Munger's response. After staring at his wife and daughter's picture for a moment, the President finally spoke.

"This is a disaster," said President Munger angrily. "The T-Rex virus stolen! How on earth could this have happened?"

Robert Jordan and the other advisors looked at each other, no one really wanted to be the one to answer that particular question. Finally, one of the military representatives spoke up.

"Well, um, Mr. President... It appears, Colonel Port was kidnapped from his home just prior to the attack. He's still missing, by the way. His identification and secret access codes to enter the facility were stolen as well. No doubt, Colonel Port was tortured into giving them away. The terrorist, apparently, used a sophisticated facial mask and pho-fingerprints designed to perfectly replicate those of Colonel Port to fool the guards."

"Son of a bitch!" President Munger exclaimed as he slapped his desk-top with his hand in frustration. "And the press already knows, too. Just what we didn't need—another international crisis!"

President Munger gestured to his laptop, where a YouTube video of Asian dictator, Jimbo Jam, was playing. In the propaganda video, a catchy hip-hop tune played as Jimbo Jam did a surprisingly well choreographed dance routine (completed with background dancers) as he rapped out lyrical warnings about global warming—while also threatening nuclear annihilation against an assortment of "punk-ass" enemies, including President Munger and the United States.

President Munger stared in amazement at the political rap video. "Jesus," he finally muttered. "We already have enough trouble on our hands with this clown, the stupid dictator of North Legeria, Jimbo Jam. This fool is actually threatening to use nuclear weapons—which he got from God knows who—against us and anyone who contributes to global warming and, by the way, will someone please tell me why the knucklehead is *rapping?* I mean, that's just so... unprofessional, even for a ruthless dictator!"

"It appeals to the millennials," said CIA director Robert Jordan with a shrug. "Jam wants the world to forget that he's a petty tyrant who brutally oppresses anyone who opposes him. He's trying to build international support for his regime by pretending to be a cool dude who seriously cares about the environment."

"You have to give the bozo some props, though," said President Munger's ambitious Chief of Staff, Wilmer Clint. "Cray-cray bastard really knows how to push his brand. His video is the number one trending on social media right now. It's even beating out your and Braungart's clip with the *'Sexiest Man Alive.'"*

President Munger slumped in his leather chair. "Wonderful, now I'm being out-polled by Dr. *Despot* Dre!"

"Maybe you should do your own music video, sir," offered Wilmer Clint. "Or perhaps you could challenge this `punk ass´ to a freestyle rap battle—like Eminem in *8 Mile.*"

"I'm going to pretend you didn't just say that," President Munger groaned.

"Anyway, sir," said the stern-faced CIA director, Robert Jordan, "getting back to our main concern here, the CIA has already made progress on the T-Rex virus case. We picked up some chatter that someone, or a group, from Chile is behind the theft."

"Chile?!" said President Munger, his voice rising a few octaves with surprise. "Since when does anyone from Chile hate us? I mean, OK, sure, there was that whole 'get-rid-of-Allende-and-put-in-a-right-wing-dictator-Pinochet thing' we did to them, but that was back in the 1970s, ages ago."

"I know, right?" said Wilmer Clint. "I mean, no one even cares about Chile in the U.S. these days, except for fourth graders who think it's the coolest shaped country in the world when they learn about it in world geography."

President Munger looked off, thinking deeply for a moment. "Gentlemen, would you please leave the room, I want to talk to the CIA director in private."

Everybody, except Robert Jordan, left the room.

"Robert, just how dangerous is that damned virus?"

"It could wipe out the entire human race, sir. That's why it's called *T-Rex,* to remind us that it could do to humanity what a comet did to the dinosaurs. That virus could easily make us all extinct."

Hearing this, President Munger looked like he was going to be sick. "So, what do we do to prevent this kind of once-in-a-lifetime super bad day? I mean, we have the virus crisis, North Legeria, not to mention climate change, pollution all over the place. We even cannot eat our fish anymore without running the risk of poisoning ourselves with lead and other hazardous chemicals. Who the hell can fix all this?"

"Braungart could," said Jordan.

Munger looked at him like he was insane. "What?! Professor Braungart. You mean the Agent-C2C-Cradle-to-Cradle-chemistry-professor Braungart? The *'Sexiest-Man-Alive'* Braungart?!"

The CIA Director nodded affirmatively. "Let's face it, Mr. President, he has better relationships with the heads of state from all around the world than you do, including that wannabe K-Pop star/dictator Jimbo Jam. Go figure."

"Are you sure?" President Munger asked incredulously.

"Yes, sir. We hacked Braungart's cell phone, and he's got the private cell phone numbers of all the VIPs on the planet... even your wife's and your daughter Peggy's contact details."

"WHAT?!" exclaimed President Munger.

"I know," said the CIA Director appreciatively.

"How did Braungart get all these personal numbers?"

Robert Jordan let out a sigh. "Well, sir, you know how it is: people like to survive. With his Cradle to Cradle design concept, he basically has a super smart, feasible idea how to avert our own extinction and us looking like the dinos, which would be vanished, drowned in our own filth, waste and shit. People get that. He's authentic, they trust him, he inspires people. I mean, just look at what the Cradle to Cradle Institute in San Francisco has achieved. Its inauguration was supported by California's Governor Arnold Schwarzenegger in 2010 in the context of the groundbreaking *California Green Chemistry Initiative*. Braungart, that man gets things going in a way we cannot, despite all our money, military force and fake news, sir. He's a genius… like Einstein."

"Hmm," said President Munger, "I never thought of him that way. You make him sound like Superman meets James Bond. And yet, when I see him, he sometimes reminds me of Mickey Mouse imitating Woody Allen. Not exactly a hero-type person."

"Maybe, but if he were to put all the VIP names from his cell on his website, he would have the maximum search engine optimization. I mean, even at the CIA, there are countless people who admire him and even suggest that we should rename the agency into EIA: Eco Intelligence Agency."

This revelation seemed to sway President Munger a bit. "Don't tell me that things like this whole, global `Fridays for Future´ movement is actually an unauthorized, clandestine, green CIA operation?!"

"No, Mr. President. Like IKEA or the Nobel Prize,

it's all from Sweden. But I tell you, today, when we try to recruit students from top U.S. universities, we have to offer them a plant-based diet program and yoga classes—twice a day. They ask things like: `Why, given that scholars like Abraham Lincoln's famed U.S. diplomate George Perkins Marsh, already warned about the destruction of the environment and climate change, like in his international bestseller *Man and Nature* from 1846, do we face all these environmental problems today.´ Recruiting is no fun anymore, sir."

"Oh, boy, things are changing faster than the news these days." The President scratched his head, frowned and deep wrinkles formed on his forehead. "Well, Braungart, he's one of the most independently thinking minds on the planet, I'll give you that. He seems like a family guy. He likes misfits who dream about a positive future. But I have a very strong feeling that he's never gonna work for the U.S. government other than telling us to install certified carpets in our buildings, which San Francisco is already doing."

Robert Jordan tossed a classified file on the President's desk.

"What is that?" the President asked.

"Just read it," replied the CIA Director.

The President looked down at the file. It was labelled "Michael Braungart". He opened the file and read through it quickly. A look of shock spread across his face.

Robert Jordan quipped: "As you said, he's a family guy."

President Munger put the file down. "You've got to be kidding me."

"It's a crazy world," replied Jordan.

"Okay…," said the President, "it might work out. But answer me this, since you've also been spying on him like hell… is his sex life really *this* good?!"

Jordan nodded. "He's the man."

Quickly, Jordan removed a flash drive from his pocket and slid it into a slot on President Munger's laptop computer. A surveillance video filmed by the CIA immediately popped up on the screen and began to play. The video showed an open back window on a house in San Francisco.

"This is Braungart's bedroom window," said the CIA Director. On the video's audio track, the excited voice of a woman could be heard crying out joyfully from Michael's bedroom window.

"Oh, Yes! Michael! Oh, my God! More. MOORE… MOOORE!"

Suddenly, a woman's sexy garment flew out of the window! It landed in a lush garden behind the house, where it joined a small collection of other women's underwear. The woman's sexy garment immediately began to fuse with the soil—just like the other garments, which were in various stages of decomposition. Jordan stopped the video. President Munger looked amazed.

"We analysed the soil in his garden," Robert Jordan explained. "It's one of the best patches of dirt on the planet: full of nutrients and positive microbes, and it stores water and CO_2. Also, his house only contains healthy Cradle-to-Cradle materials—"

"Never show this video to my wife," interrupted President Munger, "and I want a list of all the goddamn healthy, fun-promoting materials he has in his house asap."

SOMEWHERE OVER GEORGIA, USA

Meanwhile, in the first-class section of a commercial airliner, Michael and Chantal were busy enjoying the various accouchements of the VIP section. Chantal stretched out in her roomy, leather seat, sipped her complimentary glass of champagne and smiled at her boss.

"I'm so glad, you're finally doing this," said Chantal merrily. "You really do need a vacation to recharge your batteries and get some of this workload off your shoulders."

"I'm not sure if visiting my half-brother Rocky qualifies as a vacation," Michael quipped.

Chantal laughed. "So, what's Rocky like?"

"I'd say, he's less subtle than me," Michael replied with a wry grin on his face. "You'll get the whole Rocky experience soon."

"You don't talk about him much. Are you two not close?"

"Well…," Michael said, pausing for a moment to think about his response, "I love Rocky, but he's always been very busy with his import/export business. I never really understood what he was doing. But, apparently, he quit his business and wants to join me and help with Cradle to Cradle."

"That's great!" said Chantal excitedly. The champagne was starting to kick in, making her especially chatty. "Judging from my telephone conversations with him, he's very talkative. I hardly got to say a word, can you imagine? Plus, he thinks he's super funny and laughs at his own jokes, which totally ensures there are no awkward moments of silence, which I guess is a positive thing. What I'm saying is—" Chantal paused for a moment, looking confused. "Geez... what am I saying? I like totally lost my train of thought." She giggled.

Michael shook his head. Just then, Chantal's laptop let out a ding; an email had just come in. She checked the message and her face lit up.

"Sweet! A major U.S. publisher is now offering you a million-dollar advance to write a cookbook for *Generation Positive Circular Economy*, which I guess, is a new angle on cooking quality organic food and, on top of that, wait for it... a fashion label wants to hire you as a model for their new, edible spring collection! We should totally combine this and have you cook the garments on the catwalk in French! This is so freaking awesome! You're blowing up faster than dynamite!"

"Boom!" said Michael jokingly as he shared a celebratory fist bump with Chantal, but his smile quickly faded. He had more pressing things on his mind than his growing celebrity status. After all, the key question for the wellbeing of people and the planet in his mind always was: which positive quality ingredient to use in an innovative product to be *more good* and not how many toxic chemicals to reduce to be *less bad*. Unfortunately, the latter option of trying to be *less bad* was still the one most often pursued, which only meant in the long run that under the banner of *sustainability* the wrong things were made ever more perfectly wrong. Wrong products, like still toxic baby diapers, had to be burned, and their ingredients even helped the waste incineration plants, that nobody really needed, to work more efficiently. That was stupidity on crazy steroids.

Positive things, on the other hand, like baby diapers made with eco-effective, intelligent, biodegradable chemicals could be used as water storage devices in the ground to plant something like 150 trees per baby in areas where rain would normally disappear in the barren soil. Given that around 20 percent of residual waste consisted of baby diapers, it was more than obvious that redesigning and reinventing diapers based on the C2C principles would offer amazing opportunities with respect to the desperately needed reforestation in countries around the world. Based on the technology available today, it was no big deal to make most products positive anyhow and also more profitable, since, for instance, no costs for difficult, toxic waste management would occur. It wasn't morality and negative guilt management, which only resulted in aiming for being *perfectly less bad*, that was needed in the 21st century, but the joyful, holistic, all-encompassing focus on ever increasing *positive quality*.

As Chantal continued to prattle on and on about all his upcoming business opportunities, Michael's attention slowly drifted away even more. He glanced out the window of the plane and stared down at the rolling Georgia countryside below. Apprehensive thoughts of his impending reunification with his half-brother pinged around his head like a silver ball bouncing off the bumpers inside a pinball machine. For some reason, dealing with family always made the usually unflappable scientist uncharacteristically nervous.

"I haven't seen Rocky in so long," Michael thought to himself. *"I wonder if he's changed, maybe matured a little bit, probably not—he's always going to be a raging bull in a china shop. Still, if we could find a way to work together, that would be amazing. I just hope that things don't get completely out of hand, like they usually do…"*

WASHINGTON, D.C.

Robert Jordan, the CIA Director, came into the Oval Office. President Munger sat behind the Resolute desk, packing a briefcase.

"Sir, your helicopter has just landed, and Air Force One is on the tarmac at Dulles," Jordan said.

"Okay, let's do this," President Munger replied as he closed his briefcase and stood up. Just then, a Secret Service agent burst into the Oval Office.

"What now?!" President Munger demanded.

"Mr. President… Your daughter has gone missing."

All the color drained from President Munger's face. "What?! Isn't she under Secret Service protection?!!"

"Yes, of course, sir. But, apparently, she gave the two agents watching over her super-high doses of sleeping pills in a vitamin drink. She managed to slip past the security detail in the lobby, too. A security camera on the street outside her hotel in Bangkok videoed her getting into a city cab. She hasn't been seen or heard from since. We've got a plate number of the cab and are trying to track down the driver, but we really have no clue where she is now."

"Great job!" Robert Jordan hissed at the Secret Service agent.

President Munger slumped back in his leather chair, looking completely devastated. "Oh, my God, Peggy…," he groaned.

"What do you want to do, sir?" Robert Jordan asked.

President Munger thought deeply about that

question for a moment, then finally let out a deep sigh. "Well, obviously, she wasn't kidnapped, as she engineered her own disappearance. But since she takes after her activist mother: prepare for trouble."

President Munger stood up, shaking his head in frustration. He grabbed his briefcase and stormed out of the Oval Office. The CIA director turned to the Secret Service agent who was still standing there with a befuddled expression on his face.

"Well, don't just stand there looking stupid. Find her!" Robert Jordan barked angrily.

"Yes, sir!" replied the agent. He hustled out of the room, almost tripping over his own two feet in his haste.

Jordan followed right behind him, briskly speed walking to catch up with the President.

DALLAS AIRPORT

In the waiting area near the baggage claim, stood a handsome, intelligent-looking man, wearing a cowboy hat. He was in his late twenties, tan, very muscular and instantly gave off an air of being incredibly gregarious and extremely confident. This was Rocky, Michael's half-brother. In more gentile parts of the country, his bold, cocky personality would be frowned upon, but in the state of Texas, where everything was bigger and also "louder", Rocky had a hell of a lot of charm. Rocky's features only vaguely resembled those of his half-brother. In fact, it would be hard to peg the two as blood relatives at all—except for the mischievous twinkle in both their eyes.

At Rocky's side was his girlfriend, Piper, a stunningly hot, sexy woman in her mid-twenties. She was wearing "Daisy Duke" denim shorts, red leather boots and a tight, white T-Shirt. Those who knew Piper said she was sweet as molasses, unless you crossed her, then watch out! She was definitely the kind of woman who didn't take crap from anyone—which made her the perfect foil for a guy like Rocky.

As Michael and Chantal came down an escalator into the baggage area, Rocky's face broke into a wide grin. He waved excitedly and screamed out:

"That you, bro?!!!"

Michael winced slightly at the volume of Rocky's bellowing voice. Rocky stormed over to him as he continued to shout.

"Welcome to Texas, Agent C2C! Holy crap-o-la! Look at you! Your glasses are more colorful than a `Happy

Birthday´ card. And I guess, you still don't comb that Muppet style hair-do of yours. Do you even know what a barber shop looks like from the inside? Get your skinny ass over here!" Rocky grabbed Michael and pulled him into a bear hug, lifting him into the air and swirling him around. "So good to see you, Mikey!"

"Good to see you too, Rocky," said Michael, grimacing in pain from Rocky's crushing embrace. "Just remember, I'm planning to keep using my spine after it has encountered your dashing personality."

Rocky roared with laughter. "You crack me up, man!" Rocky then turned to Chantal, tipping his cowboy hat to her. "Now, h-e-l-l-o, who do we have here?!" he said, practically shouting.

"That is my assistant, Chantal."

"So, so pleased to meet you, darling. We already spoke on the phone, didn't we?!" Rocky gently shook Chantal's hand and looked deeply into the eyes. Chantal blushed.

"Yes, you're right," she said with a nervous giggle.

Rocky chuckled. "Speaking of *right*, look who's right here: my sweet, gorgeous girlfriend, Piper!"

Piper smiled sweetly and waved at everyone. "Hi, guys," she said in a gentle voice.

Michael looked shocked. "I can't believe it. You have a girlfriend who doesn't scream like you and isn't deaf already from your excellent conversational skills!"

"Man, your jokes are definitely better than my last sunburn." Rocky laughed and hugged Michael again. "C'mon, let's hit the road before I get hit by one more of your jokes. Mike, you drive with me. Chantal, you buckle up next to Piper."

Michael looked a little nervous about this arrangement. "Uh… Why are we not driving in one car?" he asked suspiciously.

A devilish grin spread across Rocky's face. "'Cause, we're gonna have some fun!"

Michael sighed, "I was afraid of that…"

CHAPTER 4

Rocky's car, a 1967 Ford Mustang Fastback, and Piper's 1970 Plymouth Road Runner came speeding down a lonely road that ran through the open Texas prairie. Behind the wheel of his hurtling muscle car, Rocky turned and smiled at Michael.

"This baby runs on Hydrogen."

"Wow. Cool!" Michael replied. "You probably want me to ask you how fast it can go?"

"Glad you finally asked." Rocky picked up a walkie talkie that was lying in a pouch on the dashboard. He clicked the call button. "Did you hear that, Piper, babe. The professor wants to know how fast these things can go."

Behind the wheel of her speeding car, Piper grinned. She clicked the talk button on her walkie-talkie.

"Heard you loud and clear, babe." Piper turned to Chantal, who was looking a little green around the gills because of the high speed. "There are barf bags in the door compartment, honey."

"Why?" said Chantal as she desperately tried to hold her breakfast down. "This is not a plane."

"Exactly." Piper replied. With that, Piper stomped on the gas pedal.

Chantal's stomach leaped up into her throat. "Oh, God…," she groaned as the Plymouth shot off like a rocket, overtaking Rocky.

Not one to be outdone by his soulmate, Rocky crushed his gas pedal, too. The Mustang took the lead. The G-force of the acceleration pined Michael to the back of his seat and made his eyes go wide with terror. Rocky glanced over at him and roared with laughter.

"How you doing there, bro? Do you need me to pull over so you can change your shorts?!!" Rocky chuckled.

"Actually, my doctor advised me recently to go about life in a more relaxed fashion," Michael replied as he clutched his seatbelt, holding on for dear life.

"If this isn't relaxing, then what is?!" Rocky asked.

Just then, a large bump appeared ahead of them on the road. There was no time to slow down or avoid it—the two cars hit the bump at full speed, which caused them to momentarily go airborne. They landed with loud thumps back on the road.

Piper squealed with joy and grinned at Chantal. "Welcome to the freedom of the open road, sister."

"I don't know if this is covered by my travel insurance," Chantal murmured.

As the two cars continued racing through the magnificent countryside, they passed a large thicket of bushes along the highway median. In the midst of the bushes was a small clearing that was impossible to see until the cars were right beside it. Two police cars were lying in wait there, perfectly hidden for a speed trap. As soon as Rocky and Piper flew by, the two police cars hit their sirens and roared out from their hiding place in hot pursuit, kicking up clouds of dust as they peeled out.

Bouncing along inside Rocky's Mustang, Michael heard the sound of the sirens and glanced into the rear-view mirror. He saw the police cars coming up fast and tapped Rocky on the shoulder.

"Uh, Rocky... I don't mean to be a buzz-kill here, but there're two police cars chasing us. In Washington, that is usually not a good sign."

Rocky, however, didn't seem too perturbed by the development. He let out a loud laugh.

"When God thought of America, he had a very good day. He wanted this to be the 'land of the free', so he bestowed upon us the blessing of fast cars and lots of open prairie to outrace our police."

Instantly, Rocky spun the wheel sharply to the right, sending the Mustang into a dangerous hairpin turn. Michael flew into the side door, bumping his head as Rocky drove off the paved highway and motored right into the open prairie!

In the Plymouth, Piper saw Rocky's evasive maneuver and grinned at Chantal.

"You're gonna love this."

"I'm pretty sure I won't...," said Chantal flatly.

Piper cranked the wheel to the right. Tires squealed and sent up a cloud of smoked rubber as she flung the Plymouth into an impossibly tight turn. Somehow, Piper managed to keep the car under control as she power slid off the highway and tore off after Rocky.

The cops weren't going to be ditched that easy, though. These were Texas cops, after all—they lived for this shit. So, the cops spun their two cars off the highway and bounced onto the bumpy prairie, spilling coffee and donuts all over themselves. This made them very pissed off and even more committed to chasing down Rocky and shoving a nightstick up his ass.

In Piper's car, Chantal stared straight ahead, wide eyed. Too terrified to move. Her fingers were dug deeply into the upholstery as she watched Piper step on the gas and follow Rocky's car straight towards the edge of an oncoming cliff, preparing to jump it.

"Michael said you wouldn't be subtle, but this is just insane!" Chantal screamed.

"Why do you always sound like you're having a nervous breakdown?!" Piper said as the rim of the canyon hurtled towards them.

"Because I am!"

Piper just shrugged and gripped the wheel. The Plymouth and Mustang flew off the rim of the canyon, one after the other… and landed safely on a plateau on the other side.

The police jammed on their breaks and skidded to a

stop on the far side of the cliff. The cops exited their cars, covered in coffee and donuts, cursing angrily and vowing vengeance.

Rocky glanced back at them in the rear-view mirror, chuckling to himself. "At least in their reports they can say, they had each other covered: with coffee and donuts!" He roared with laughter at his own bad pun and slapped Michael hard on the shoulder. Michael wasn't as amused.

"You know," he observed dryly, "there are more sophisticated ways to avoid police contact, like driving like a normal person."

"What's awesome about that?!"

Meanwhile, inside the Plymouth, Piper looked at Chantal, concerned—her passenger was turning greener than a fresh Texas chili pepper.

"How do you feel, sister? You do look a tad bit queasy."

Chantal shook her head. "I'm totally fine," she said with a faint smile. Then, suddenly, her face went completely pale. She snatched up the barf bag, stuck her entire face in it and hurled her guts out.

Rocky and Piper zoomed up and screeched to a stop in front of a beautiful country estate. Michael stepped out of the Mustang looking very much like a man who was just thankful to be alive. As he took in Rocky's sprawling house, he noted the presence of an extra-large, pink balloon in the shape of an elephant attached to the roof.

"What the heck is that about?" Michael wondered to himself.

Rocky, Piper and Chantal (slowly) exited the cars. Overflowing with joy, Rocky threw his arms wide and gestured excitedly at his residence.

"Will you look at this place, bro! Is my home the shit or what?!!"

Michael nodded, genuinely impressed. "Yes, it looks totally amazing, Rocky."

"It's even better than that. This crib has it all!" Rocky shouted. He then began counting off its many virtues on his fingers. "Breath-taking views, my own courtyard, pear-, apple-, walnut- and cherry trees, water features, a humongous swimming pool with a waterfall, pastures, numerous old barns and outer buildings! This is country paradise!"

"I didn't know that there was an extra, super-large pink elephant in paradise," said Michael with a smirk.

"I'm glad you haven't lost your sense of humour." Rocky chuckled. He glanced over at Chantal who looked like she still hadn't recovered from the drive, yet. "Are you O.K., honey?"

Chantal shook her head and repressed a gag. "I feel a little seasick."

"From that little spin in the car?!" exclaimed Rocky, flabbergasted.

Piper came over and helped Chantal to stand up straight.

Rocky, meanwhile, proudly pointed at the pink elephant floating over the main house. "That, my dear brother, is the official logo of our new company. It's called 'Pink Elephant' and do you know why?"

Michael thought about it for a second. "'Cause the anatomically incorrectly shaped elephant is so embarrassed?"

"Nope, sugar face," Rocky replied, "because it's a super cool name. You said, *'thinking of zero waste is like thinking of a pink elephant.'* So, I turned the whole thing around. Thinking of our company 'Pink Elephant' means thinking of Cradle to Cradle products. I think this is gonna be a real crowd-pleaser!"

"You're kidding, right?" asked Michael incredulously, "I mean, I hope you're kidding—are you?"

But Rocky just shook his head as he began escorting Michael towards the house. "No, I'm dead serious. I quit my old export/import job, and together with Piper, I founded the internet company 'Pink Elephant' that sells only C2C products. I'll tell you all about it in a minute."

Rocky whipped his head around and glanced back at Chantal and Piper. "How's it going back there, sailor?" Chantal gave Rocky an uncertain look.

Piper took her by the arm. "Let me help you. Can you walk, darling?" Piper asked sweetly.

Chantal nodded and took a cautious step forward, but immediately clutched her stomach. "I think, I'm going to be sick."

"Again?!" Piper said with a laugh. "Are you sure, you're not just pregnant?"

Chantal shot her an angry look.

"I'm just kidding. C'mon, let's get you inside so you can decompress. Down here in Texas we always say: 'After a long hard day, there's one thing that makes everything better—'"

"I'm praying you're not about to say, 'Tequila.'"

"Nope, it's something even better…"

Once inside the mansion, Michael, Chantal and Piper sat around a large sectional sofa in Rocky's spacious living room. Rocky entered the room from the kitchen, merrily whistling a popular country tune. In his hands, he held a serving tray with tall glasses filled with ice tea. He passed the drinks out to everyone and then raised his glass high in the air for a toast.

"Here's to long overdue family reunions and meeting new acquittances!" he said with gusto before taking a big swig of his tea. Chantal and Michael looked down at the glasses of ice tea with dubious expressions on their faces. Rocky saw their hesitation. "Go on, kids, don't be shy. I promise, this time—*I did not pee in it*."

"He really did that once," said Michael, rolling his eyes at the memory of the incident.

"What can I say? Shit happens," Rocky chuckled.

"Don't worry, he's matured since then," said Piper. "I've been house training him. He even puts the toilet seat down now."

Chantal stared at the glass of ice tea. Finally, she took a small, hesitant sip. Her expression instantly changed from suspicion to surprise.

"Wow… that's actually pretty good," she exclaimed.

Rocky beamed with pride. "Ha! Told, yah, girl! It's my own special brew." He turned to Michael, "C'mon, bro, whatcha waiting for?"

Michael exhaled and took a little sip. He also looked pleasantly surprised. "Hmm… a little tart, maybe, but it's actually not half bad."

"Yeah, yours might be a little sour, 'cause I did put a little drop of wee-wee in it—just for old time's sake."

Michael made a face.

Rocky laughed hard again and affectionately patted him on the leg. "Relax, I'm just messing with ya, bro!"

"I knew that," said Michael, even though, he sorta didn't. As he continued to sip his ice tea, Michael took a moment to survey the expansive room. It was decorated with an odd juxtaposition of Dallas Cowboy sports memorabilia and an eclectic mix of art from around the world.

"You have very… interesting decorating taste, Rock," Michael remarked as he eyed a rare Chinese print that was hanging on the wall next to a football helmet signed by Roger Staubach.

"Definitely," agreed Chantal. "Where'd you get all this stuff?"

"Here and there," Rocky replied with a shrug. "I used to travel a lot for my import/export business. It gave me a golden opportunity to collect art. You like?"

Both Michael and Chantal nodded enthusiastically.

"You know, Rocky, I have to admit, I'm really surprised," Michael said. "I mean, look at you, fancy house, settling down with a gorgeous woman, selling Cradle to Cradle products on the internet. It's like, you've grown up overnight, or something. I like it, but it's a little strange."

"How so?" Rocky inquired.

"Well, you loved your export/import business. I never understood exactly what you were shipping around. But, whenever I tried to contact you, you were out of the country, hanging out in places I didn't know existed. You said you were very happy, though, and couldn't imagine living any other way. Then, all of a sudden, boom! You drop it all. I just don't get it."

"There is nothing permanent except change," Rocky replied.

"Now I've heard it all: Rocky quoting Heraclitus. How cool is that?!" said Michael.

Rocky seemed genuinely touched by the compliment. "Thanks, bro."

Just then, Michael caught something odd out of the

corner of his eye. Through the living room window, Michael suddenly saw numerous black SUVs racing up to the house. The cars skidded to a stop in the driveway. Dozens of armed men dressed in black suits, wearing dark sunglasses jumped out of the vehicles and started marching towards them.

"This doesn't look good," Michael thought to himself. "Speaking of cool," Michael said, gesturing to the window, "are you a member of some kind of large Blues Brothers' tribute band, or organizing a 'Men-In-Black' reunion?"

Rocky turned and looked out the window—his jaw dropped. "What the hell?!" he shouted.

Rocky jumped out of his chair and hustled over to the front door. Piper, Michael and Chantal followed behind him. Quickly, Rocky swung his front door wide open just as several of the "Men In Black" arrived at his doorstep. Their faces were taunt and showed no emotion whatsoever.

"Can I help you?!" Rocky demanded.

The man nearest to Rocky flipped open an ID badge with the official U.S. seal on it. "We're Secret Service," he said in a no-nonsense tone of voice.

"But I'm not the President," Rocky replied, sounding confused.

"That's right," a second agent chimed in. "But he'll

be here in a minute."

"No shit? The prez is coming here?" asked Rocky in amazement.

Just then, the loud whomp-whomp-whomp sound of an approaching helicopter could be heard. Rocky and the others stepped out of the house and looked up into the sky. The President's personal helicopter, Marine One, came into view, hovering right over their heads! The copter flew to an open spot on Rocky's huge front lawn and landed. Rocky turned to Michael and excitedly exclaimed:

"Holy crap! I can't believe this, bro. It's freaking Marine One!"

"Interesting," said Michael rubbing his chain, "I wonder what this all about." Chantal furrowed her brows, not sure what to make of this strange development.

"Well, it must be something pretty damn important for President Munger to show up in person," said Piper. "He doesn't usually make house calls."

"Either that, or they take reckless driving really seriously around here," Michael quipped.

A few moments later, President Munger, the CIA director, Robert Jordan, Rocky, Michael, Piper and Chantal were sitting together in the living room.

"Would you like some ice tea, Mr. President?" Rocky inquired.

President Munger shook his head politely. "No, thank you."

"You should try some," said Michael. "It tastes really great, especially the ice."

"As tempting as it sounds, Professor Braungart, I didn't come here for refreshments."

"May I ask, why we are honoured with your presence, sir?" Rocky asked.

President Munger studied their faces closely for a moment, then continued: "What I'm about to tell you is highly confidential, classified, top secret information." Munger gestured at Michael and Rocky. "As such, I'd prefer to share what I have to say in private with just you two gentlemen."

Rocky instantly shook his head. "Sorry, Mr. President, but I tell Piper here everything—she's my bae. You know what that means, right?"

"Not really," said the President flatly.

"It means we're soulmates," Piper interjected.

"As in, bound together for all eternity, what's hers is mine, the whole nine yards," Rocky said. "I can't keep secrets from her."

Michael also shook his head. "Chantal is my personal assistant. She has my complete trust. I share everything with her as well. She stays, too, it's non-negotiable."

President Munger looked irritated. He glanced at the CIA Director.

"It's your call, Mr. President," said Robert Jordan.

"Alright, very well," the President finally said. "But if any of this is leaked to the press... I'll have you all thrown into Guantanamo."

Chantal gulped. Rocky didn't seem too fazed, though.

"What's going on, sir? Has your dog, Pauline, gone missing again?" he asked with a smirk.

"No, but my daughter has," President Munger replied. "But that's a whole other story, *this* is the main reason we came here today..."

The President nodded at Robert Jordan. The CIA Director opened up a laptop and set it down on the coffee table in front of the group. On the screen, a video played, showing the masked international criminal/terrorist, Alex Torex, stealing the T-Rex virus. Then, a mug shot of Torex's face without the custom-made latex mask appeared on the screen.

"Gentlemen...," Jordan began to say, but Piper and

Chantal coughed. Jordan corrected himself, "Ladies and gentlemen, this is the world's most wanted terrorist, Alex Torex from Chile. Recently, as our intel has revealed, he stole our most lethal, top secret biological weapon, a super-virus we call the 'T-Rex', by pretending to be the missing Army Colonel Harrison Port. In a couple of days, Torex is planning on selling the virus to the highest bidder at an auction at his villa in Brazil."

"So, why don't y'all just send in an elite commando team and take his sorry ass out like y'all did with Bin Laden?" Piper asked.

"Love to," replied Robert Jordan. "But unfortunately, Brazil isn't Pakistan. We had some leeway to go after terrorists like Bin Laden there, because their military needed our foreign aid. The Brazilians don't. Sending in official U.S. military personnel could be interpreted by the Brazilians as an act of war and set off an international incident."

"Plus, there's the damn media to think about," President Munger added. "The situation is bound to get leaked to the press if we go through official channels. We'd like to keep this thing on the downlow, if at all possible, to avoid panicking the public." Michael looked very confused by all of this.

"What does this have to do with us?" he asked. "Despite the rumour that I have everybody's private cell phone number, I certainly do not have Mr. Torex's."

"We know that," said the CIA Director pointedly. "What we also know is that there's a high probability that the T-Rex virus is being stored in a safe somewhere inside Torex's villa."

"Sounds reasonable," observed Piper.

"Wonderful, we're all on the same page then," said Jordan. "Anyway, it just so happens that Mr. Torex is a huge fan of renewable energies…"

"A gangster terrorist with an environmental conscience?" marvelled Rocky. "Isn't that what politicians are supposed to have, too?"

Jordan ignored the ironic comment. "Our plan is to send in covert operatives to break into the heavily guarded villa, replace the vial containing the virus, and then wait until all the potential buyers arrive to arrest them in a joint operation with Brazilian forces as soon as they cross the border."

Rocky nodded approvingly. "Great plan! Round 'em up and lock 'em all away. The more the better, I say. And while you're over there, tell your special ops team to take a little detour and stop by Italy—at least that's what I always did after… my successful business trips. You really need some downtime once in a while. It's proven, it's all science. That's, by the way, how I met Piper. Seriously, Italy. I tell you, you should really try the Formaggella del Luinese, it's the best goat cheese in the world. I mean, the Italians, they have that whole slow food thing going strong." Rocky turned to Michael. "Right, bro? It's like the land of kicking back on the porch with some red wine, pasta and goat cheese."

Michael opened his mouth to say something, but President Munger jumped in, looking back and forth between him and Rocky. "Wonderful, then the two of you will really enjoy a side trip to Italy once you're done with the operation."

Both Rocky and Michael's faces dropped.

"Say what now?!" Michael sputtered.

"We want the two of you to go to Brazil," Robert Jordan said.

"But I don't speak Portuguese," Rocky protested. "I mean, I know that model/actress Alessandra Ambrosio is from Brazil, and I could ask her for her phone number. But that's it."

"Good for you," Piper sneered.

"I would, of course, only ask Alessandra for her

phone number to give it to you, Piper, so that the two of you could go shopping—as best friends."

"Obviously," Piper replied, frowning at Rocky.

"Wow, smooth. I really liked how you just side-stepped your relationship minefield there," said Michael shaking his head.

"Ladies, gentlemen, please!" President Munger exhaled.

"Oh, before I forget. Can I also call bullshit on this whole Brazilian idea?!" Michael added.

"We figured," Jordan replied. "But since Torex is obsessed with renewable energies, Professor Braungart should easily connect with him, which should get the two of you into Torex's villa." Jordan gestured at Rocky. "Once inside, you Rocky, with your extensive CIA background and part-time job of checking the driving skills of the Texas police on behalf of the government, should have no problem figuring out a way to exchange the vial containing the virus."

Michael was stunned. He turned and stared at Rocky with an incredulous expression on his face. "You have a CIA background?!" Michael said, astonished. "That's not exactly a low-key truth bomb!"

Rocky looked embarrassed. "I'm not a friggin' spy!"

"So, you never worked for the CIA?" asked Chantal sceptically.

"No!" Rocky insisted. Then, he bit his lip and said in a soft voice: "I mean, yes, I sorta, kinda, maybe I did. I mean... well, it's a secret. I'm no longer with them. I quit. I just sometimes test the preparedness of the local police force." He gave Robert Jordan an angry glare. "Why you gotta out me like that, bro? I thought you were cool."

"I love this," said Chantal, amused by it all. "This is better than group therapy."

Michael continued to stare at his half-brother in amazement. "You do know, the CIA isn't a humanitarian organisation?"

"It could be worse."

"How exactly?" demanded Michael. "It's the freaking CIA! It's Jurassic Park out of control!"

"Excuse me?!" said the CIA Director indignantly.

Michael ignored him and continued berating Rocky. "CIA, huh?! That's what you called your import/export job?"

"Yeah, well, I suck at cover stories," Rocky said defensively. "Cut me some slack, bro. Lots of agents make up these big, elaborate stories to hide their undercover work from their family and friends. I always thought, *'hell, that's kinda disrespectful.'* You know what I mean? Like, if you gotta bullshit people, at least go small, right? So, I kept it vague and simple for you."

"How thoughtful," Michael replied sarcastically.

"Look," said Rocky, his voice rising with emotion, "I'm really sorry. I didn't want to deceive you, Michael. But let's be fair, bro, you don't really come around to visit much. You're always so dang busy jet-setting around the world, trying to save the planet from an environmental apocalypse, that you never really cared what the hell I was up to. It made me feel kinda bad that we had grown so far apart. That's why I left the agency and wanted to get in-volved in your C2C stuff, so we could be closer—like real, full-on bros saving the world together."

Michael didn't have an instant comeback for that. He had to admit that Rocky did have a point; he didn't re-ally care that much about Rocky's business ventures—who was he to judge him for lying about it?

Across the room, Piper leaned over to Chantal and whispered to her: "You're right, this is fun."

"Come on," Rocky pleaded with Michael. "Let's combine our superpowers like the Wonder Twins! You're known worldwide as Agent C2C. So, we're practically on the same page."

President Munger sighed, he was getting a little impatient with all the family drama. "Gentlemen, please...," he started to say, but Michael interrupted him.

"I'm speechless, Rocky, like that pink elephant on your roof top, or when I first heard of the idea of becoming carbon neutral, because this only works if humans and this planet do not exist." Michael's blood was boiling now, words just tumbled out of his mouth. "We are not too many people on this planet, we are just too damned stupid! We constantly try to minimize the wrong things instead of doing the right things. Ants have about the same biomass as humans or even more, but they do not produce waste. We, on the other hand, produce tons of toxic waste no other species can use. That's just insane!"

President Munger nodded eagerly. "I agree wholeheartedly, professor. That's exactly why we want you to help us. Please, do the right thing."

"I am not working for the CIA," Michael insisted.

"Of course not!" President Munger replied. "You wouldn't be working for the CIA, or the U.S. government because this conversation, right here, *never happened*." President Munger winked at Michael.

"I very much wish that was true," Michael said glumly as he buried his face into the palms of his hands in exasperation. The revelation that humanity was on the brink of destruction, *and* the discovery that his half-brother was leading a double life was overwhelming.

Rocky walked over and patted him on the back, trying to comfort him. "Hey, Mikey, come on. I always admired you—you're my hero. If that virus gets into the wrong hands, it could wipe out all of humanity. Is that what Agent C2C would want to happen?"

"At least we'd be sorta carbon neutral then," Michael replied stoically.

"Professor Braungart, seriously," President Munger said solemnly, trying to sound as presidential as he could, "I completely understand your objections. But if this plan works, we could arrest the most dangerous criminals on the planet, all at once."

Michael didn't respond—nothing it seemed would move him.

Then, suddenly, a light bulb went off in Rocky's head. "Wait a second here, folks. I just got a brilliant idea!"

"Oh, God, here it comes...," Michael groaned.

"What if, in exchange for our services, the President made sure that at least twenty new Cradle to Cradle chairs were established at major universities across the U.S."

Michael's ears perked up.

"What?" cried President Munger in shock.

"You're right," said Rocky, "that's thinking *way* too small. Go big or go home, am I right? I'm seeing two hundred Cradle to Cradle chairs all across America!"

"Are you insane?!" growled President Munger.

"Hey, three hundred chairs are a fair deal, sir," Rocky retorted.

"But you just said *two hundred,*" corrected the President.

"If three hundred is not enough for you, fine!" said Rocky with a grin. "We can make it four hundred."

"Two hundred Cradle to Cradle chairs!" Robert Jordan chimed in.

"Whose side are you on?" President Munger said, sounding very annoyed.

"I'm very sorry, sir," Robert Jordan replied, respectfully, "but this might be the only chance for me, as the CIA Director, to ever do something reasonable. Besides, one of your predecessors, U.S. President Bill Clinton, wrote the foreword to Braungart's and McDonough's second book *The Upcycle.*"

"Wow, that's deep, man," Piper observed.

All eyes turned to Michael now. Everyone was staring at him apprehensively as they waited to see what his decision would be. Michael leaned back in his chair and closed his eyes, trying to think clearly. The room fell silent, the only sound was the steady ticking of an old pendulum clock that hung prominently on the wall above Michael's head. The tense moment seemed to last forever.

Finally, Michael nodded. "Brazil it is."

Rocky pumped his fist and shouted: "Yes!"

Piper let out a loud "whoop!" and slapped a high five with Chantal—who, in spite of her outward excitement, looked a little unsure about the whole adventure.

The President and Robert Jordan looked at each other, and both breathed a sigh of relief...

CHAPTER 5

DALLAS INTERNATIONAL AIRPORT

Michael and Rocky hustled quickly through the bustling airport, heading for their airplane. As they arrived at the security check point, Chantal and Piper waved good-bye to them. Michael and Rocky waved back, as they removed their shoes and put them in the grey plastic bin to be scanned by the TSA.

"Man, I'm so excited about this trip to Brazil!" Rocky bellowed. Then, he added at even a higher volume:

"I mean, we are about to be cooler than James Bond!"

"And definitely louder," Michael remarked.

Soon, the boys were in the air, flying south over the Gulf of Mexico, on their way to Brazil.

PRESIDENTIAL PALACE, NORTH LEGERIA

Meanwhile, halfway across the world, inside a beautiful suite in the secluded palace of North Legeria's dictator Jimbo Jam, the U.S. President's wayward daughter, Peggy Munger, was fussing over an important decision: should she wear the *pink* or *blue* traditional kimono that Jimbo had sent to her room. She was genuinely torn; the pink one, which was decorated with large cherry blooms was definitely the prettier of the two. However, the blue one went with her eyes. *"Hmmm...,"* Peggy thought to herself, *"I kinda like both of these, but is either one really going to get me to the finish line here...?"*

After some debate, Peggy suddenly had a great idea. She dug a special item out of her backpack, put it on, and then she slipped the pink kimono over it. Suddenly, there was a loud knock. Peggy opened the door to her room and found herself facing two large, unsmiling, armed guards.

"Our dear leader is awaiting you," said the lead guard in a deep, accented voice.

"Wonderful," Peggy replied with a sly smile.

She trotted out of the suite, wearing silk slippers and headed down the hallway, accompanied by the two guards. Her escorts lead her down several corridors in the maze-like palace until they finally arrived at an enormous, luxurious dining room. The high walls were decorated with countless pieces of art from all over the world; giant, green plants stood next to the tall windows, and one super large pop art painting displayed Jimbo Jam doing his rap routine. The slightly pudgy dictator/wannabe rapper, Jimbo Jam—wearing expensive hip hop clothes/streetwear, golden bracelets, rings and necklaces—sat at the far end of the very long, wooden dining table, pensively drinking an expensive brandy. He immediately rose to his feet when he saw Peggy enter.

"Ah, Mrs. Munger. What a true delight!" he said with a warm smile, obviously enamoured by the stunning natural beauty that was wrapped up so neatly in the lovely pink kimono. He hustled over to her in his untied, diamond embroidered sneakers with crossover lacing (worthy of a real hype beast), bowed politely, took her hand and kissed it.

"It's a pleasure meeting you."

Peggy blushed slightly and returned his greeting with a traditional Asian bow. "You're so kind. I'm tremendously honoured, your Highness," she said, batting her eyes daintily.

Jimbo's heart skipped a beat. He gestured to a seat beside his at the oversized dining table. "Please, join me for breakfast, won't you?" Jimbo escorted Peggy to her place at the table.

A stone-faced waiter wearing white gloves and a spotless black tuxedo appeared out of the alcoves. He stepped forward and gently pulled Peggy's chair out so that she could sit down. As she took her seat, Peggy subtly opened the knot of the obi ribbon that kept her delicate kimono in place.

The traditional garment slipped off her body and fell to the floor, revealing a short, red, sexy dress underneath. Jimbo Jam let out an audible gasp. His eyes bulged. If this was an old Warner Brothers cartoon, his tongue would literally have popped out of his mouth like Daffy Duck and rolled half across the floor.

"If you don't mind," Peggy said casually, "I feel more comfortable in somewhat lighter clothes."

The stoic waiter quickly picked up the discarded

kimono and retreated. Jimbo stared at Peggy lasciviously for a moment as drool accumulated in his mouth. He was completely overwhelmed by Peggy's amazing looks.

"I-I can see, Mrs. Munger," he sputtered, "that you are full of lovely surprises and have impeccable taste."

"And I'm glad, you're a man who appreciates the completely unexpected."

"Indeed, I am!" cried Jimbo as he plopped his chubby butt down in his seat. He gestured to the large breakfast feast spread out on the expansive table before them. "Please, enjoy!"

"My, my, my...," said Peggy, "will you just look at all this incredible grub!" Peggy surveyed the magnificent mountain of breakfast edibles which included several styles of eggs, stacks of waffles & pancakes, whole slabs of bacon, piles of different sausages, bricks of hash browns, trays with salmon carpaccio, countless brands of cereal and an assortment of fresh fruit from around the world. It was enough food to feed breakfast to half his starving population.

"Fresh strawberries are the best!" Peggy said with a grin as she reached for an extra-large, red strawberry in a golden bowl in front of her.

As Jimbo watched in utter amazement, she picked

up a super huge strawberry and licked it gently up and down with her nimble tongue, savouring its sweet skin before taking a slow, seductive bite out of it. She played with the bite in her mouth, swishing it back and forth with her eyes closed before finally swallowing and letting out a blissful moan, "Ahhh..."

Jimbo was so enthralled by her performance that his fine motor functions betrayed him, and he actually dropped the fork he was holding, which clattered loudly on the table. Across the room, Jimbo's guards stared at Peggy with their mouths wide open. The unsmiling waiter, who was walking by with Peggy's kimono, hissed at them in a harsh, low voice:

"Close your mouths!"

The two guards immediately shut their gapping pie holes and went back to looking like emotionless, intimidating thugs.

UNITED NATIONS BUILDING, NEW YORK

Halfway around the world, it was just turning dusk in New York City. The lights inside the iconic United Nations building were starting to turn off one by one. The building never really closed for the night, but it was mostly quiet now as the majority of the world's diplomats and their staff had left for the evening.

Inside the magnificent edifice, however, there was, at least, one person who wasn't going anywhere this evening. He was a stout man in his mid-thirties, dressed in a military uniform. In his sweaty hand, he held an envelope marked *classified*. He clutched it tightly as he rushed down a secure hallway deep inside the United States diplomatic wing. Finally, he arrived breathless at an office door that was marked UNITED STATES AMBASSDOR.

The sweaty man hurriedly placed his thumb on a keypad outside the door. A scanner quickly read his fingerprint. Instantly, a beep indicated that his identity was confirmed as a green light lit up on the ID sensor pad, and the door unlocked. The sweaty man hustled inside the office. Once in, he walked briskly past the busy secretary who sat outside the office of the U.S. Representative to the United Nation, Barry Hogan. Without bothering to knock, he burst into Hogan's office.

Barry Hogan, a middle-aged career diplomat, looked up, somewhat surprised by the intrusion. The sweaty man held out the classified message to him.

"It just came in, sir. You have to see this."

Ambassador Hogan took the envelope from him and quickly opened it. He surveyed the contents, and his face went pale. Inside the envelope was a photo of America's first daughter, Peggy Munger. The picture was taken inside what appeared to be a dungeon. She was chained up to a wall wearing a white nightgown that was torn apart in many places. Her once pretty face was dirty, emaciated and full of stress. Rats could clearly be seen, running around her feet. In the picture, Peggy looked sacred and frightened. Hogan stared at the picture in horror and shouted out to his secretary:

"Get the President on the phone immediately!"

RIO DE JANEIRO, BRAZIL

It was a beautiful evening. The glowing lights of the incredible, dazzling (and sometimes dangerous) metropolis of Rio shimmered brightly on the tranquil waters of Guanabara Bay. A white limousine drove down the glitzy Avenue Atlantica that flanked the world-famous Copacabana Beach and pulled up to the entrance of the five-star Arts & Gardens Hotel. It was the city's iconic, architectural Art Nouveau masterpiece that included decorative elements inspired by nature in its overall design, be it the interior walls of the building, its furniture, the glass art of its windows, textiles or metal work. The Grand Hotel had welcomed and entertained guests from around the globe since 1900. The limo doors opened and out stepped Michael and Rocky, wearing sunglasses with manually adjustable darkeness, looking more like rock stars than undercover spies. Rocky threw his arms wide and turned around in a 360-degree spin, like he was presenting the city to Michael.

"Behold, bro… Rio!" Rocky said triumphantly. "The seventh wonder of the modern world. Is this blowing your freaking mind or what?"

"Naturally," Michael said with a smile. "I've been here many times, and probably you as well."

"True that," Rocky exclaimed, "and I'm so glad to be back!" Rocky turned around and looked at the famous beach only footsteps away from the hotel. "Last time I was here on a world-saving, action-packed business trip, I wasn't able to fully hit the beach during daytime and enjoy the fun. You know what I said to myself back then?"

"Oh, please tell me."

"Well, since you're asking. I said to myself: 'I should definitely focus more on inhabiting the moment with the help of the national Brazilian sign language.'"

"What's that?" asked Michael.

"Samba!" Rocky shifted his body into the wiggling Samba mode. "Can you feel the rhythm?!"

"Hey, Mr.-life-of-the-party! Boy, you're really a natural talent for everything. You should so put Samba dancing skills on your resume." Michael rolled his eyes.

Just then, the limo driver turned to them as he unloaded their suitcases from the trunk. "Excuse me, sir," the limo driver asked Rocky, "but would you like me to take your bags into the lobby?"

"The lobby would be awesome, my man!" said Rocky with a big toothy grin.

Once they entered the spacious lobby—illuminated by glittering chandeliers and decorated with numerous, beautiful, large flower arrangements in delicate glass vases—Michael and Rocky sauntered the shiny marble tiles over to the reception desk. An elegant female receptionist in her late twenties, named Ana, greeted them.

"Boa noite," she said in a voice that sounded like melting butter.

"Boa noite," said Michael, "my name is Braungart, Michael Braungart."

Ana's eyes instantly lit up at the sound of his name.

"Ah, senhor Braungart! Greetings!" she exclaimed. "We've been expecting you. I hope you had a pleasant trip."

"Yes, we did, thank you." Michael gestured to Rocky. "This is my brother, Rocky, also from the U.S."

"How you doin', darling?!" Rocky declared.

"Very well, thank you," Ana replied warmly. "I'm delighted to welcome you both as our very special guests. Here are your key cards to the Presidential suite. It comes with a red C8 Corvette Convertible."

Rocky's jaw hit the floor. "Man, that's 495 horse-power!" he cried out in astonishment. "The C8 is the new hotness of the Vette family. Besides the humanity's-story-arc-changing experiences of apple pie and baseball, this intense energy machine is the true meaning of awesome. It effortlessly transcends age and culture. That's why America's sportscar is the most popular sportscar in history; not to mention, this sweet menace is equipped with a road-legal 6.2-liter V8 mid-engine—60 mph in less than 3 sec, of course—and it displays the most elegant body modifications ever! Holy, WOW!"

"Indeed, senhor Rocky," Ana said with a wink, "she's one sexy beast!"

Then, in a very graceful fashion, Ana handed the key cards to their room and the Corvette keys to Michael.

Michael looked down at the room key; the words "Suite Presidential" were spelled out on the top of the card in bright gold letters.

Michael furrowed his brows in confusion. "I'm sorry, senhora, I don't mean to look such a lovely and charming gift horse as yourself in the mouth, but there must be some kind of mistake. We only booked two regular rooms with king sized beds."

"The suite is a complimentary upgrade from our hotel," Ana replied. "We are honoured to have the *'Sexiest Man Alive'* staying with us, Professor Braungart, or should I say 'Agent C2C'?! Our manager is an enormous fan of your work. He wanted me to tell you personally that he was particularly impressed with your groundbreaking pilot projects here."

"Projects?" said Rocky looking at Michael surprised. "You never told me you were doing projects down here."

"It's nothing, just a little stuff I've been trying out," said Michael humbly.

"You're too modest, Professor," Ana interjected. She looked at Rocky, "He and his team designed a groundbreaking, incredible system where C2C concepts are used to recycle wastewater in our subtropical regions. He helped build facilities that conduct biomass nutrient recycling so that wastewater is not just dumped into the rivers, or the ocean, but treated and purified so that nutrients are recovered, and the purified water—a byproduct—can then be released back into the environment or used in agriculture. His system turns wastewater into useful resources, enables local farmers to produce more valuable, nutritious, organic produce, enhances biodiversity, and provides safe drinking water to poor communities at very little cost. He even included the participation of school children to help build and monitor the facilities."

"Wow, that's amazing!" said Rocky, his voice brimming with admiration. "I'm so friggin' proud of you, bro! Just one simple idea: Eliminate waste from the beginning and everything can get circular and positive on the entire planet. That's smart!"

Michael just smiled shyly as he replied: "We actually expanded the eco-intelligent Brazilian project all over South America and brought it to China as well. It's only just a few pilot projects here and there—putting people, profits and planet on a mutually beneficial and positive track. I hope we can do much bigger things in the future."

"Me, too," said Ana. "And by the way, all our staff members wear compostable clothes here. If there's anything I can do for you, professor, please don't hesitate to call upon me." Ana handed Michael her personal business card.

"Thank you, senhora," Michael replied as he took the card. "I'm always delighted to meet people who have a mutual interest in composting clothes..."

Ana laughed. "It's Ana, for my friends."

"Nice to you meet you, Ana," Michael said with a twinkle in his eye.

"My clothes dissolve, too, by the way, just in case you were wondering," Rocky chimed in.

"I'll make a note of it," Ana said playfully. "The elevators are right over there across the lobby. You'll need that key card to access the penthouse. The bellhop will meet you up there with your luggage."

Michael and Rocky turned and walked away from the reception desk. As they headed towards the elevators, Rocky peaked over his shoulder and caught a glimpse of Ana watching them walk away. They got into an open elevator, and Michael pressed the key card against the control panel which unlocked the access to the penthouse suite. As soon as the doors shut, and they were alone again, Rocky turned to Michael.

"Man, was it my imagination or was that mega-hot receptionist, Ana, totally checking you out or what?! I mean, you had the whole James-Bond-flirting thing going for you back there. Did I ever tell you how proud I am of you?"

"Yes, Rocky, about half a second ago."

"But did I *also* mention how you owned the whole freaking room when you wiggled your flat ass into that hotel lobby? Man, you are simply beyond brilliant, even with your eternally fuzzy hair and those color-screaming glasses on your face."

"You want the key to the Vette, don't you?" Michael sighed.

"Holy shit! And you can read minds, too! Can you get any more amazing!"

PRESIDENTIAL PALACE, NORTH LEGERIA

10:00 AM. As the mid-morning sun rose high in a cloudless sky, the beautiful Palace Gardens were an island of peace and serenity in the busy North Legeria capital. In fact, the only sounds that could be heard across the expansive grounds, that were arrayed behind Jimbo Jam's enormous Presidential Palace, was the occasional rustling of leaves from a gentle breeze and the melodic chirping of several species of local songbirds. The Garden's unique design was based upon Chinese Taoist traditions and was intended to promote tranquillity and meditative contempla-tion. On top of a gate that led to the entrance to a large temple located in the heart of the garden, was the ancient *Neijing Tu* diagram; an intricate picture that dated back thousands of years which depicted the human body as a mi-crocosm of nature.

On the ground in front of the temple, was a large Yin-Yang symbol made from large slabs of black and white marble. Next to the symbol was a small, manicured pine tree and an Asian-style Zen fountain that featured tiered mini-waterfalls which dispensed water softly in four oppo-site directions, each one representing one of the four cor-ners of the Earth.

Peggy Munger stood in the middle of the Yin-Yang symbol. She was in very deep concentration, breathing slowly with her eyes closed, as she methodically moved her body through a series of complex and fluid Tai Chi poses. Peggy was dressed in traditional Tai Chi clothes with a white jacket held together by three red strips of cloth that went all the way up to her throat. The temple area was sur-rounded by a ring of 10 intimidating guards, all wearing full parade uniforms, who were facing away from Peggy.

As Peggy went through her exercises, a sweet, lyri-cal chirping sound suddenly met her ears. Peggy's eyes fluttered open, and she saw, directly in front of her, a beautiful red-tailed Minla bird, sitting on one of the branches of the manicured pine tree, considering her. Peggy took a deep breath and moved in slow-motion into a difficult Karate-Kid-like pose with her arms spread wide, palms up, while she stood on one leg with the other raised leg curled behind her. She smiled at the little Minla bird and slowly closed her eyes.

Amazingly, as if it somehow picked up on her "at-one-with-nature" vibe, the Minla flew to Peggy and landed in her out-stretched, open hand! Peggy opened her eyes again and smiled at the little visitor chilling in her palm. Suddenly, Peggy let out a faint gasp, her pretty eyes rolled back in her head as she was struck by a powerful vision. It was like a waking dream, but it felt very real and totally vivid.

In her mind's eye, Peggy could momentarily see inside the bird's eye; which opened up like a huge window to reveal a panoramic view of the cosmos with its infinite galaxies and stars. As she continued to watch in amazement, Peggy saw the solar system with all the planets, orbiting the sun. Her visualization then zoomed in on planet Earth, descending downwards through the atmosphere, passing over continents, oceans, then a large Asian city where it zeroed in on a Taoist garden until she could finally see herself in the Karate-Kid-style Tai Chi pose from a viewpoint floating just above her own body.

Then, as quickly as it came, the vision abruptly ended. The Minla bird chirped at Peggy once more and flew happily away. Peggy stood in her pose for a moment, contemplating the miraculous epiphany she'd just experienced. Intuitively, she had the sudden sense that she was being watched. Peggy looked over to the large Presidential Palace, where…

… from an upper floor window, Jimbo Jam was observing Peggy through a pair of binoculars. Jimbo, again looked more like a rapper than an autocrat, dressed as he was in a flashy Fubu jump suit complimented by copious amounts of bling: golden necklaces, bracelets, rings, etc... The door to Jimbo's private office swung open, and a chubby, middle-aged servant with a sunny, submissive smile permanently etched onto his face, entered. The man approached President Jam and bowed so deeply that his forehead almost touched the floor.

"Dear leader, dear sun of our people, dear spirit keeper of the land…," the supplicant sang out in a reverent voice dripping with honey. Jimbo cut the sycophant off with a raised hand.

"Get your fat face out of my butt. What do you want?"

"Of course, dear marvelous, most wise, and beautiful leader, so sorry to interrupt your important bird-watching time, but we are ready to execute shooting you."

"Oh, snap!" Jimbo cried. He took one last ogling look at Peggy, then tossed his binoculars aside. "Let's do this shit, yo! It's showtime!"

A short time later, Jimbo was on a sound stage, waiting impatiently as a nervous makeup artist hurriedly applied the final touches of cosmetics to his face. He was standing in front of a giant green screen, wearing designer sunglasses, a tank-top and baggy trousers that hung half way down his backside. Whenever Jimbo changed from "dear leader" to being "the hot performer", everyone had to call him by his short, cool, two-letter code of power nickname: "JJ". Milling around behind him was a group of a dozen cheerleaders, all of whom were dressed in short skirts and military-uniform tops.

Peggy was there, too, perched on a special VIP director's chair, sipping on an organic smoothie as she reviewed images for the green screen with the editing team.

She shook her head firmly "no" when the editor showed her a picture of the Buddha with Jimbo's face photoshopped over the Enlightened One.

"Nope. Not working for me. It needs to be more subtle… Go with the Dharma Wheel—that's what I saw in my vision." The editor nodded and swapped the images.

"You feeling the background pics, baby?"

"Yeah, JJ, everything looks dope. I made a few small changes, but you'll dig it, trust me." Jimbo flashed a sideways peace sign at Peggy.

Finally, the makeup artist had finished her job. She held a mirror up so Jimbo could see himself. "Dear glorious leader, do you approve?"

Jimbo gave his reflection a quick glance. "Yeah, yeah, great job, I look like a stud, as always. Thanks!"

The makeup artist bowed and rushed quickly off set. Jimbo lifted up a megaphone to his lips and bellowed out to the director, and the rest of the crew assembled on the sound stage.

"I'm ready, fools, let's get this shit rollin' already, yo!"

Everyone nodded dutifully and hustled to their various positions. The nervous director glanced around to make sure everyone was set, then he cupped his hands on either side of his mouth (since Jimbo had appropriated his mega-phone) and shouted out:

"Action!!!"

The infectious, thumping backbeat of Jimbo Jam's Hip Hop song rang out on the playback. Peggy bopped her head and moved her hips to the beat. The backup dancers began moving through an odd-ball dance routine that combined twerking with aggressive martial arts combat moves and fancy military parade-style high-stepping and synchronized rifle twirling. The dance number, which had been choreographed personally by Jimbo, managed to look sexy, ridiculous and threatening all at the same time.

As the dancers gyrated their collective booties behind him, Jimbo lip-synched to a special remix version of his infamous hit song, repeating the chorus "The Jimbo-Jam Chi—Yeah, Yeah! The JJ-Whooppee—Yeah, Yeah!" many times both in English and in his mother tongue.

Images displayed on greenscreen behind Jimbo showed pictures of the five animals of Feng Shui: the Tiger, the Dragon, the Snake, and the Turtle all merged together to become the Phoenix that raises again. This was followed by a picture of the golden Dharma wheel hovering inside an upside-down, heart-like shape—flanked by two identical, golden, kneeling deer—that morphed back and forth between a huge close-up of Jimbo's face and a Yin-Yang symbol that radiated like the sun.

As the last notes of the song faded away, Jimbo, screaming "JJ-Whoopeeeeeee!", dramatically dropped his mic on the stage and struck one final, defiant *gansta-style* pose with his arms crossed in front of himself.

"And cut!" yelled the director.

The room fell silent. No one dared say a word. Everyone waited for their President-turned JJ to react, but he just stood there in his gangsta pose with a stone-cold poker face. Jimbo finally glanced over to Peggy.

"What say you, boo?"

"JJ, JJ! That was kinda freaking dope!" she said with a smile. "I love it!"

"Fuck, yeah!" Jimbo shouted. "Me, too!"

The entire crew and all the guards instantly burst into wild applause and cheering. Crew people threw their arms around each other, hugged and kissed each other like it was New Year's Eve. The director, certain he'd been spared from a trip to a firing squad, flopped on the ground and began doing "the worm". The cheerleaders were so overcome with raw emotion that they were crying uncontrollably. Everyone was fawning over Jimbo, calling him a genius and congratulating him profusely.

Jimbo made his way through the celebration over to Peggy. When he got to her, they stared deeply into each other's eyes. Jimbo lifted up his hand and gave her a gentle "dap".

"We're the *Dream Team*," she said with a grin.

Up in the surveillance and control center of the palace, there was a whole different breed of individuals watching the widely entertaining moments of the music video shoot with JJ. The meanest and most sinister guy in the room was the hardliner and "I-dust-you-all" general named Takeshi (which, no surprise, meant "fierce"). He was the creative minister of the interior and the big boy of the security apparatus of North Legeria (the citizens snidely called him "head of housekeeping").

While most of JJ's staff tried to look both alert and happy (like room service, ready to nice you to death), he exclusively looked alert and super angry, as if he had put too much hemorrhoid cream on his face. The "I-will-cut-down-the-bullshit-factor-in-the-palace" expression in his devilish eyes gave away the fact that he intensely disliked what he had just seen on the flickering surveillance monitors...

RIO DE JANEIRO, BRAZIL

Bright and early the next morning, Rocky and Michael sped away from the Arts & Gardens Hotel in the hot, red Corvette. They roared off down the Avenue Atlantica, turning heads as they thundered off through the streets of "The Marvellous City". Before long, they had left Rio far behind and were racing due south along the picturesque Brazilian coastline. The big and beautiful Brazil itself was, by scientists around the world, considered to be the country with the largest biodiversity. Michael was always impressed and amazed to discover that many exotic plants and unique birds chirping in the most special ways. Even Rocky stepped off the gas once, when they spotted a magnificent whale appearing not far from the coast bursting out of the water.

"Do you know why whales actually live much longer than mice or humans?" asked Michael.

"Because… they exercise more?"

"No, because they are bigger. Their metabolism runs much slower. So, they get to stick around a lot longer. There's actually a mathematical formula—"

"Whoa, whoa. Let me stop you right there, sparky,"

Rocky interrupted. "Math is not my thing. I once tried to count all the bikini models on the beach. I tell you, when you get to number three, the whole concept of mathematics gets very blurry. I think it's because of the bikinis, since they're so hard to locate, like a distant galaxy—far, far away."

"Yeah, bikinis can be a tricky, cosmic math challenge."

"See. I'm so glad we talked this through—like adults. Because now, we're one mind again, see eye to eye, are on the same page, where it says in huge bold letters: ACCELERATION!" Instantly, Rocky stepped on the gas again, and the Vette roared further south.

Their destination was a rugged three-pronged peninsula in one of Brazil's most famous bays at the Costa Verde—around 96 miles south of Rio—that lay just beyond the city of Angra dos Reis. This beautiful locale was home to some of the world's greatest beaches, with marvelous, turquoise ocean water and a sought-out place for diving between coral reefs, shipwrecks and a stunning, exuberant marine fauna. But, more importantly, it was also the location of a villa that was secretly owned by a certain international terrorist named Torex.

The boys drove less than an hour, enjoying the

incredible views as they motored down the spectacular coastal highway, until Rocky finally parked the Corvette on a hilltop overlooking a beautiful villa. A large, yellow scorpion quickly crawled away as Rocky and Michael got out of their car to take a look around. The sprawling, luxury estate sat in the middle of a very exclusive, secluded area that featured residences owned by very wealthy individuals from all around the world. This particular, splendid, modern-looking mansion, equipped with granite walls, the latest smart windows and solar panels, a panoramic terrace, large swimming pool and jacuzzi and embedded in palm trees, was isolated from neighbouring compounds by acres of tropical forest, where one could see monkeys hopping around the trees. Rocky quickly checked coordinates on a briefing map that Robert Jordan, the CIA director, had given them. He scratched his head and pointed down at the property.

"I think that's Torex's crib right down there," said Rocky.

"Are you sure?" Michael asked.

Rocky shrugged. "Kinda, sorta... hell, I don't know. All these fancy-ass estates look the same to me."

"You think, perhaps, it would be a good idea to figure that out?!" Michael suggested, trying hard to hold back his rising frustration.

"Yeah, probably. Tell you what, let's just kick back here awhile, enjoy this perfect scenery and wait." Rocky reached into the glovebox and pulled out a Cuban cigar.

"Wait? Wait for what?!" Michael cried. "For Torex to pull out a big bullhorn and announce: 'Here I am you fucking dim-wits!'"

"Chill-lax, bro," Rocky replied calmly as he lit his cigar and took a big puff. "*The Rock* has it covered."

Just then, a beat-up old Fiat sedan with a surfboard attached to a roof rack pulled up beside them.

Rocky looked surprised. "Wow, he's on time for once."

Inside the Fiat was a tan, muscular Brazilian man in his mid-forties. At first glance he looked like a beach bum with his mane of shaggy brown hair and a stubbly beard. As he sprung out of the Fiat, Michael noted that he was wearing a beat-up old pair of shorts and flip-flops. Rocky let out a hearty laugh. Michael watched in amazement as Rocky and the stranger immediately threw their arms around each other and embraced like two long-lost chums.

"Marcos! Long-time no see, amigo!" Rocky bellowed.

"Tell me about it, you crazy son-of-a-bitch!"

Marcos replied exuberantly. "What the hell, Rock? I thought you were enjoying your CIA retirement."

"I was, but plans changed, thanks to my brother." Rocky gestured over to Michael.

Marcos turned to him and shook his hand firmly. "Professor Braungart," he said politely. "It's an honour to meet you. I think your books are fantastic."

"This means you have at least read two books," Michael replied. "That's good for the fast-growing intelligence of the CIA community."

"Good one, professor," Marcos chuckled.

Rocky put his arm around Michael's shoulder. "He's always so generous with his inspiring praise." Rocky then turned to Marcos again. "So, buddy, what have you got?"

Marcos pulled out a pair of binoculars from the passenger seat of his Fiat and surveyed the beautiful villa below them. He nodded and then handed them over to Rocky.

"It's that gem down there all right."

Rocky peered through the binoculars. "Man, that villa sure doesn't look like a dying spinster."

"It's one of the finest estates in this area," Marcos observed. "Very heavily guarded with a state-of-the-art surveillance and the latest off-grid solar electric power system."

Through the binoculars, Rocky could now see dozens of armed guards patrolling the estate with vicious-looking attack dogs at their sides. "Nice," he muttered. "Perfect for family vacations and illegal business gatherings of all kind." Rocky handed Michael the binoculars. "Take a look, champ. Just like I told you; that's Torex's cosy little hacienda, where he's expecting all his scum-bag homies to drop by for the big auction. That's where we will be going tomorrow."

Marcos took an iPad out of his car. He tapped the screen, and a blueprint of the villa appeared. Michael and Rocky leaned over and took a gander at it.

"The room with the safe containing the vial with the virus, we think is here, on the second floor."

Rocky studied the layout and looked concerned. "Hmmm... not a lot of easy access points. That's gonna be a tough nut to crack."

Michael, meanwhile, had spotted something with the binoculars; guards were unloading a large box on the patio near the swimming pool.

"It looks like they're setting something up near the pool," he said.

Marcos nodded affirmatively. "They've had huge packages delivered all morning. Tomorrow is Torex's 50th birthday."

As Michael continued to watch, he spotted a handsome man with a moustache dressed in a grey jumpsuit, stroll out of the main house. He appeared to be giving orders to the other men. "I think, I just spotted Torex," Michael said.

"Lemme see," said Rocky.

Michael handed him the binoculars.

"Yep, that's him alright," Rocky confirmed. "Let's make sure *tomorrow* will be a birthday he never forgets."

Suddenly, the thundering roar of a fast-driving motorcycle met their collective ears. All three men spun around and saw a Harley Davidson barrelling right towards them! Too stunned to move, they just stood there, frozen like statues, as the badass hog did a daring, stunt-like power slide. It came to a screeching stop right in front of them, kicking up a cloud of dirt. Michael waved his hands in the air and coughed.

As the dust settled, they saw that the Harley's driver was wearing an all-black leather riding outfit with a racing helmet covering the head. The motorcyclist considered them for a moment, then pulled off the helmet to reveal a familiar, lovely face; it was Piper! She greeted the boys with a big smile punctuated by a loud snap of her chewing gum.

"Hiya, boys!" she declared.

Rocky, Michael and Marcos looked at each other in bewilderment, totally surprised at Piper's sudden appearance.

"Holy shit, baby doll!" Rocky blurted out. He rushed over to Piper and gave her a big kiss. "You really know how to make a freaking entrance!"

Michael was less sanguine about the surprise development. "What, why?" he stammered.

Piper ignored his query for a moment as the Corvette caught her eye. "Is that a smoking hot Vette C8 I spy with my little eye?!"

"Hell, yeah!" Rocky shouted triumphantly. "And Uncle Mike let me drive it!"

"You, lucky bastard! I hate you!" Piper growled as she playfully punched Rocky in the arm.

"Again: Why—" Michael started to say before Piper cut him off.

"You kids didn't really think I would let you pull this off all by yourself, did ya?" Piper turned to Marcos. "Ola, Marcos, nice to see you, buddy. How's it hanging?"

"Piper Emmy Geller," Marcos replied as a knowing smirk spread across his face. "Good to see you again on another extraordinary mission."

"Let me guess...," Michael started again, trying to put it all together.

"Yep!" Rocky interjected. "She's a kick-ass computer scientist from MIT. She's also a marine biologist and training to be an astronaut—"

"—and I'm with Interpol," Piper added.

"Right, Interpol," said Rocky. "And she's an expert chef."

"Ahhh," said Michael wistfully. "That's why the two of you can make such great, *spicy* ice tea. Mind-blowing."

Piper took the binoculars out of Rocky's hands and peered down at Torex's villa. She surveyed the estate for a moment or two, then let out a squeal of delight.

"Love it! Love it! Love it! This is sooo the place for hug-all girl."

Rocky shook his head, looking scared. "Piper, no. No 'hug-all' girl!"

"I'm so gonna be Hug-All!" Piper insisted. "If you're gonna steal something, *steal the show as well*." She laughed and gave Rocky a big kiss. "Love you!" With that, she handed the binoculars back to Rocky and jumped onto her Harley. She started the engine and gunned the throttle.

"Sweet dreams, boys!" she shouted above the bike's roar. She put on her helmet and raced off, popping an insane wheelie as she raced down the road.

Rocky grinned from ear to ear as he watched her disappear. "God, I love that crazy lady!" he declared.

The next day, at noon, driving in Marcos' non-descript old Fiat, Rocky, Michael and Piper, approached the Torex Villa. Rocky parked the vehicle around 100 yards away from the expansive estate, just beyond the range of Torex's extensive surveillance equipment. As Piper took out the binoculars and did a final survey of the main compound, noting its many surveillance cameras and solar panels, Rocky turned to Michael.

"Okay, Mike," Rocky said, "one last tip from the world of spies: If you get afraid, fart."

"What?" Michael replied dubiously.

"I know it sounds wacky, but trust me, these criminals are like animals. If they smell fear, it triggers their predatory response reflex, and they pounce. So, you gotta give them something if you get too scared to distract their reptile brains. That's where SSF, or *Serious Smelly Farting*, comes in."

"Seriously?"

"Absolutely," Piper chimed in as she slipped behind the Fiat and began adjusting her hair. "That's part of 21st century chemical warfare. You've no idea how many times Rocky and I farted ourselves out of a deadly, dead-end situation."

"Sounds like solid spy psychology," Michael observed dryly.

"And one more thing," Rocky added, "don't get into your priceless Ted Talk routine. Let the gangsters talk. Numb-nuts villains are notorious ego-maniacs by trade, they love to hear their stupid thoughts out loud."

"Wow. Who would have guessed?" Michael replied.

Suddenly, Piper called out from behind the Fiat. "Done! How do I look?!"

Rocky and Michael turned around. Piper stepped out from behind the rear of the car. She had fixed her hair up in the most ridiculous way: a French braid on top of her head, complimented by braids on either side of her head. The silly doo looked something like Princess Leia meets Euro-trash hillbilly. To keep her hair in place, Piper used funny looking hair clippers with endings in the shape of ladybugs. The sight was so peculiar, that Michael was momentarily struck dumb and couldn't speak.

"Oh, my God." Rocky purred. "*That* is pure genius,

boo!"

The three climbed back into the Fiat and drove the last 100 yards towards the villa. Once they were just outside the front gate, Rocky parked the car on the other side of the road. Rocky and Michael grabbed a pair of cameras lying on the backseat. Michael started to exit, but Rocky stopped him momentarily.

"And one more thing, bro: for the next two and a half minutes, be really freaking loud as hell!"

"So, just act like you in other words," Michael said.

"Perfect!" Rocky replied as they ambled out of the car.

Michael, Rocky and Piper had all changed their clothes, now they all wore cheap T-shirts, baggy shorts and flip-flops. Rocky reached back into the car and turned on the Fiat's radio. A samba song wafted out of the speakers, Rocky turned up the volume to the limit and let the loud music blare out of the open car door. Piper instantly started hugging everything she could put her arms around: street-lamps, trees, the car, Michael, Rocky. Meanwhile, Michael and Rocky started taking pictures of her crazy antics, while making very loud, ad-lib remarks to express their fascination with the building.

"This villa is like sooo epic, dude!" Rocky shouted as he snapped a photo. "Brazil is AWESOME!!! These pics are going right up on my Instagram page! My homies back in Lubock are gonna be like so jealous!"

"Totally, brah!" Michael screamed as he took a selfie of himself smiling and flashing a peace sign in front of the front gate. "YOLO, BITCHES!"

At that moment, in the heart of Torex's villa, inside a secure, high-tech surveillance room, two guards stared intensely at Michael, Rocky and Piper dancing around like idiots on their security monitors.

"Fucking tourists!" one guard muttered to the other.

The other guard shook his head in annoyance. They continued to glare with cold, hard expressions chiselled on their rough faces as Michael and Rocky attempted some very lame Samba dance moves that were totally out of sync with the music. The boys then slapped high-fives and waved directly into the camera mounted on the front gate. While they continued their ridiculous routine, Piper kept up her insanity bit, hugging everything in sight like she was high as a kite on ecstasy. The eccentric performance was starting to make both of the guards a little uneasy—they didn't know what to make of it exactly, but whatever it was, they didn't like it.

"Get the boss!" the lead guard ordered.

The second guard nodded and quickly left the room. The remaining guard watched on the monitors as Rocky pulled off his cheap T-shirt and whirled it around in the air over his head like a male stripper. Rocky tossed the shirt aside with a stylish flourish and struck a sexy pose, flexing his muscles in front of the house as Michael snapped photos of him.

"I think I'm gonna be sick," the guard muttered.

Just then, Alex Torex entered the surveillance room followed by an unusually short, but very muscular man. His name was Bruno, he was Torex's head of security.

"What the hell is going on?" Torex demanded.

"These idiots, they dance and take pictures of the house," the guard replied gesturing at a monitor where Piper could be seen wrapped about a Braúna tree. "And that one keeps hugging everything like it's the pope."

Torex and Bruno eyed the unwelcome visitors on the monitors warily.

"I wonder who they are?" Torex wondered aloud.

"Two men and a crazy woman," offered one of the guards.

"I can see that!" Torex replied angrily.

Bruno shook his head, he looked very concerned. "We need to get rid of them immediately, boss," Bruno finally said to Torex. "They might be harmless fools, but it's best not to take any chances. We should probably send a couple of men out there to dispose of them quietly. Should I give the order, boss?"

Torex didn't respond at first, something had caught his eye. "Wait… Hold on…," he finally said as he zoomed in on Michael's face. "I recognize that one. That's Professor Michael Braungart!"

"Who?" Bruno asked.

"You know, Michael Braungart, the famous chemist…? The co-founder of Cradle to Cradle…? The '*Sexiest Man Alive*'?!"

Everyone suddenly got it, they all nodded their heads in unison and let out a collective cry of "Aaah!"

At the front gate, Rocky and Michael continued their sexy photo shoot, while nearby, Piper hugged the mailbox. Suddenly, the front door of the Torex villa swung open. Torex himself, guarded by Bruno and two of his men with Doberman Pinschers, appeared. Rocky gave Michael a subtle wink. Michael smiled and waved to Torex.

"Ola, senhor, what a wonderful villa you have!

Sorry, I hope we're not disturbing you. We're just having a bit of fun in the sun out here. We'll turn the music down." Rocky went to the Fiat and turned down the volume as Michael strolled over to Torex, extending his hand in a friendly manner.

"Do you speak English, senhor? I am—"

"—Professor Michael Braungart from Washington," said Torex, finishing his sentence.

"Oh, wow, you know me?"

"Anyone who cares about the planet knows you, Professor Braungart," Torex replied with a warm smile. He glanced over at Rocky and Piper. "And who are these two?"

"That's my brother, Kevin Plouff from Texas," Michael replied. He then pointed at Piper who was still attached to the mailbox, "... and we call her 'Hug-All'." He leaned in close to Torex and whispered: "She's got *issues*."

Piper grinned at them with a crazed look on her face and suddenly let go of the mailbox. She ran towards Torex and threw her arms around him, hugging him tightly. The dogs barked and snapped at her furiously. Bruno and the other guards drew their guns.

Rocky rushed over, waving his hands frantically. "Easy, boys! Please, don't shoot!" he pleaded. He turned to Torex, "Sorry, amigo! She's like an octopus, she hugs everything—even her dentist." Rocky wagged a scolding finger at Piper and spoke to her like an overly excited puppy. "No, Hug-All! Bad girl! Down! Leave it!"

Piper sniffed Torex and made a grossed-out face. "You smell like mommy when she's asleep."

"What?!" Torex said.

"Again, I'm so sorry!" Rocky said, prying Piper off Torex.

As Rocky disentangled her, Piper snapped her chewing gum loudly in Torex's face. She then took the wad of gum out of her mouth and offered it to him. "Want some?" she asked innocently.

Torex just stared at the saliva covered gum, disgusted.

Rocky took the wad of gum from Piper and popped it back into her mouth. "You keep that," he ordered. Then, Rocky turned back to Torex. "She also loves sharing everything. We better get her meds going before she offers you her underwear!"

"Not wearing undies today," Piper announced merrily.

"TMI, baby, let's not get into sharing details, okay?"

Torex and his men looked at each other, slightly

amused.

"Yes, she definitely needs her meds, right away," Michael said to Rocky. He looked at Torex. "I'm so sorry to trouble you, senhor, but we really need to give Hug-All her afternoon medication, would you happen to have a spare bottle of water handy?"

Bruno immediately shook his head. "We can't—"

But Torex cut him off mid-sentence. He patted Michael on the shoulder. "Of course, professor. Why don't you come inside? After all, it's not every day that I get to meet a preeminent eco-warrior scientist such as yourself. I'd love to chat with you about your work and pick your big brain a little. That is, if you have a moment or two to spare."

"That's so very kind and generous of you, Senhor!" Michael replied cheerily. "Yes, of course! I'd love to chat with you about C2C. I'm always incredibly excited to explain my concepts to a receptive mind."

"Excellent," Torex said. "Follow me."

He gestured towards the open front gate. As everyone began moving towards the villa, Piper stared at the bodyguards' guns, looking confused. She whispered something into Rocky's ear. Rocky shook his head.

"No, that's not the men's loaded tiny, little thing, honey."

133

"Potato?" Piper said, hopefully.

"No, it's not their potato either," Rocky sighed.

"Tomato?"

"No, it's a gun. It has nothing to do with vitamins."

"That sucks...," said 'Hug-All Girl' looking very disappointed.

Torex's palatial villa was spread out over several acres of coastal rainforest. There was a half dozen buildings on the sprawling property, but the main house was a giant two-story structure which wrapped around an enormous salt-water pool. The architectural style of the edifice was ultra-modern, yet ergonomic which made the entire estate both luxurious and at the same time, totally compatible with the surrounding, natural environment. In spite of his obvious desire to bust Torex, Michael found himself genuinely impressed with his quarry's aesthetic taste.

As soon as they entered the main house, Piper let out a squeal of joy. "Walls!" she cried in a high-pitched voice. She rushed over to the white, stone walls of the entryway and started hugging them with both hands.

Michael looked at Torex with an embarrassed expression on his face. "Sorry, I forgot to warn you, she's crazy about hugging walls..."

"Especially ones on the 2nd floor with any kind of wood panelling," Rocky added, "We think it has something to do with Tourette's Syndrome. It started happening ever since we visited this jungle tree house in Costa Rica. Do you happen to have any colorful paintings in your villa?"

Torex shook his head. "No, why?"

"Uh, it's nothing," Rocky replied, sounding relieved.

"Nothing?" Bruno inquired suspiciously.

"Well, it's just that she sometimes tries to eat paintings off the wall. She thinks they're large fruit roll-ups. Once she tried to eat a Picasso off the wall of a museum in Barcelona. It's... It's...," Rocky's voice quivered as his eyes teared up. "Hug-All... She's so...," Rocky stopped and covered his face dramatically. "I'm sorry, it just gets to me sometimes."

Michael patted him on the back sympathetically. "It's okay, Kevin, we all understand. Love is always a heavy burden to bear, especially when the ones we care about are batshit crazy."

"Thanks, bro," Rocky said, wiping a tear away.

The bodyguards looked at each other and shook their heads dismissively. Torex just shrugged. Suddenly, a big grin spread across Piper's face. She disengaged from the wall and started running up a nearby staircase.

Rocky called after her. "Say 'Hi' to Santa!" He turned to Torex, "She never breaks anything when I say that, 'cause she loves wintertime."

"But, it's summer," Torex observed.

Piper stopped dead in her tracks and turned around with a crazy look in her eyes. "What did you just say?!" she demanded.

Rocky quickly put a finger to his lips and shushed Torex. "Shhh. Good Lord, man!"

"Did he just say it was summer?" Piper growled, raising a suspicious eyebrow.

"Of course not, sweetcakes!" Rocky said, chuckling nervously. "All the nice man said was, 'Christmas without carols is total *bummer*!'"

"It is...," Piper said thoughtfully.

There was a moment of awkward silence, then Rocky suddenly started singing: "Jingle Bells, Jingle Bells..." He used his hands to conduct the song, then nodded at the others, encouraging them to join in.

Michael, Torex, Bruno and the other bodyguards started to sing along, too. "Oh, what fun it is to ride in a one-horse golden sleigh—hey!" They warbled together. After a few off-key verses, a smile returned to Piper's pretty face.

"That's better!" said Rocky, sounding very relieved. "Now run along and go say 'Hi' to Santa, sweetie."

Piper giggled and bounced up the stairs, whistling "Jingle Bells" as she went. Rocky and Michael breathed heavy sighs of relief.

Michael turned to Torex. "Let's go outside quietly where we can talk and get some water for Hug-All's medicine."

Torex nodded. He gestured to one of his guards. "Keep an eye on her!" he ordered.

All five men then carefully tiptoed their way through the house and headed out a back door. Torex escorted Michael and Rocky onto his porch that had a perfect view of his huge pool and beautiful gardens and, of course, a stunning panorama of the Atlantic Coast. The pool area was filled with beautiful bikini models. Torex made a sweeping gesture with his hand and smiled proudly.

"Welcome to my lovely home."

"May I just say: Wow! Holy Cow!" Rocky said enthusiastically.

Michael nodded in agreement. "Very impressive, Mr. Torex, terrific view."

"Please, Professor Braungart, call me Alex," Torex

replied. He pointed at numerous solar panels that were arrayed on the roof all the buildings around the property and a row of wind turbines on a nearby hill. "As I mentioned earlier, I am very familiar with your work, professor. As you can see, I am a big fan of renewable energies. We are proud to produce all our own energy here."

"Yes, indeed, you've incorporated many wonderful, innovative ideas on your estate," Michael observed. "That's why we stopped to take pictures. I want to show my students how people from all over the world are implementing technology to harvest renewable energies."

Torex looked genuinely gratified by Michael's comments. "I am honoured, professor. Come, let me show you my new, flexible solar panels. I'm sure you'll find it fascinating."

"Lead the way, Alex!" said Michael with a smile…

Meanwhile, inside the main house, "Hug-All Girl" aka Piper, was skipping merrily down a hallway, singing Christmas songs. The slightly bemused guard was trailing behind her. As she waltzed through the mansion, Piper passed by a long corridor that led to a metal door at the end of it. The door was adorned with multiple high-tech locks. Piper knew instantly that this was Torex's office.

Piper stopped singing and stared at the door. She tried to take a step into the hallway that led to it, but the security guard immediately grabbed her by the arm.

"Stop!" he said sternly. "That area's off limits."

"Why?" Piper asked innocently, then, she lowered her voice, "Is that Santa's workshop down there?"

"That's right, bebe," the guard said with a condescending smirk. "All the elves are working hard behind that door, making presents. We wouldn't want to disturb them now, would we?"

"Oh, *hells* no!" said Piper, shaking her head emphatically. "Bugging elves is a sure-fire way to end up on the naughty list. That actually happened to me once. I told a teeny-weenie little lie, and look what I found waiting for me in my stocking on Christmas morning…" Piper reached into her pocket and pulled out a large black rock. "A lump of coal!"

"Ah," the guard said chuckling, "how sad."

"Tell me about it," Piper replied with a long face. "The thing is," she said, leaning in very close to the guard, "I can't help it. I like to tell little white lies…"

Suddenly, Piper snapped her head forward, headbutting the guard! The impact made a sound like a coconut being hit with a hammer. The guard staggered backwards, momentarily stunned from the surprise blow. Before he had time to recover, Piper spun her arm around in a big circle like a softball pitcher and clocked him on the back of the head with the "lump of coal". The guard went down instantly, knocked out cold. Piper looked down at him and sighed.

"Sorry, Santa… I guess, I'm just a *bad, bad girl.*"

With that, Piper took out one of her dragonfly shaped hair pins. She pushed a tiny switch on the back, activating it. The dragonfly's wings united together, producing a screen that illuminated through ultraviolet light a tangled web of alarm-triggering hidden laser beams that secured the corridor leading to Torex's office. Piper removed a small pouch from her pocket, opened it and poured a little mound of white powder into the palm of her hand. She took a deep breath and blew the powder into the air. The floating thin dust drifted down the hallway, making all the laser beams visible to the naked eye.

Piper studied the configuration of the laser sensors for a moment or two, and then, did a serious of insanely acrobatic, twisting contortions as she managed to slip around each beam to reach Torex's office. Halting in front of the door, Piper now took out another one of her hair clips, the one that was shaped like a ladybug.

Piper turned one of the ladybug's antennae, and the back of its shell opened up, revealing a pair of tiny wings. The artificial insect took off from her hand and flew right into the door's keyhole. Seconds later, a series of tiny clicks could be heard, and a green light appeared on the security keypad. Piper gently pushed the door open and slipped quietly inside...

Meanwhile, down at the pool—filled with some fancy guests and surrounded by further shady looking out-of-towners—Torex's husky guards and busy staff prepared for a big party. A young woman, wearing a tiny Leopard bikini, strolled up towards Torex and his two new friends. She had a body-building's physique and a sharp look in her eyes.

"This is Tina," Torex said, gesturing to Michael and Rocky, "she's the chief compliance officer at my company." Then, turning back to her, he said: "Tina, this is Professor Braungart and his loud brother Kevin Plouff from the U.S."

Tina smiled and shook Michael's hand so hard that his eyes bulged. "Welcome, Agent C2C."

"Thank you, ma'am," Michael replied in a strained voice as he struggled to hide the discomfort of having his hand crushed. Tina smirked and gave him a sexy once-over before moving on to hob-nob with other guests.

"As you can see, your reputation as Agent C2C precedes you, professor," Torex said with a smile.

"Your compliance officer makes a big impression as well," Michael replied, rubbing his aching hand. "She gives a whole new meaning to the words *augmented reality*."

Upstairs in Torex's office, Piper carefully closed the door behind her and quickly scanned her surroundings. The spacious room had a small balcony that offered a picturesque view of the estate through the branches of a tree, but the office was surprisingly understated for a meglo-maniac's base of operation. A simple modern-style glass and metal desk along with matching chairs were the only furniture. A few pieces of well-chosen art from various indigenous Brazilian tribes adorned the walls for decoration, and there was a large, colorful abstract painting—resembling an exploding nose, Piper thought—hanging on the far wall behind Torex's desk. But there was no sign of a safe, or anything that could hide something important in the room.

Piper looked up, and she spotted a surveillance camera strategically mounted directly above her head, pointing into the room: one step forward and she'd be on 'Candid Camera' for sure. Piper quietly removed another dragonfly pin from her hair. She engaged a switch on its belly, and the dragonfly fluttered out of her hands and landed atop the camera above her head.

The microdrone lifted its long tail over itself and pointed it at the housing of the surveillance camera. A tiny laser beam shot of the tail and deftly cut a small hole into the camera's metal skin. The machine insect removed the cut piece with its tiny legs, reached inside and began fiddling with the device's circuits.

After it was done changing a few wires around, instead of filming live footage, the surveillance camera began transmitting a still image of the empty office to the guards in the surveillance room—the guards glanced casually at the monitor that showed Torex's "empty" office, totally unaware that anything was out of order.

Now that the camera had gone "dark", Piper walked towards the large abstract painting hanging on the wall on the far side of the room like a messy, colorful accident. Reasoning that this must be significant, since the surveillance camera was pointing at it, Piper reached behind the painting and began feeling around the wall…

Back at the pool, Torex, Michael and Rocky strolled over to a large group of tables shaded by big sun umbrellas. The tables were covered with numerous, incredibly expensive, items; priceless jewellery, designer clothes, high-end electronics, rare objects of art, etc... Each item was decorated with a colorful bow. In the middle of the gaudy display was a table that featured a very large, elaborately decorated birthday cake. The confection had several layers built on tiers and featured an amazingly accurate bust of Torex himself, made with chocolate cake, icing and butter cream. The massive dessert was surrounded by a huge stand filled with gourmet cupcakes.

"Are you celebrating your daughter's sweet sixteen?" Rocky remarked glibly as he subtly dipped his finger into the frosting of one of the cupcakes.

"No," Torex replied, sounding a little offended, "I turned 50 today, and we're gonna have a big party tonight to celebrate."

"Congratulations," said Michael.

"Thank you, professor. But I have to admit," Torex said with a mischievous grin, "I couldn't help myself, I opened up a few presents already." Very proudly, Torex pointed over to several large tables; dozens of the very latest high-tech remote-control drones were spread across them. All the drones were painted bright gold and were equipped with sophisticated cameras.

"Sweet!" Rocky exclaimed excitedly. "You have your own mini-air force—that's so freaking cool!"

"Yes, they're a gift from Hungnulu Kondulu, the President of a little, very legitimate republic in Central Africa."

"That's a quadcopter pilot's wet-dream, bro!" Rocky declared sounding a touch jealous.

"What an irresistible collection," Michael added.

"Indeed," Torex said looking a little frustrated. "Yet, somehow, they won't fly."

"Are you kidding?!" Rocky cried. "They were meant to do nothing but fly."

"We tried to start them all morning," Torex said with a shrug. "But strangely enough, no matter what the heck we tried, we just cannot turn them on."

Rocky smiled and patted Michael on the back. "Well, if that doesn't sound like an emergency for our professor here."

"Me?" Michael blurted out, caught off guard.

"Of course, you're the smart one here, aren't ya?" Rocky replied sarcastically. "People who are named *Kevin Plouff* sure don't know how to handle remote control drones."

Torex looked at Michael with a hopeful, pleading expression on his face. Michael exhaled and glanced at the drones, wondering quietly in his mind how the hell he was going to get out of having to tinker with them.

At that precise moment, back in Torex's office, Piper's probing fingers finally found a small button hidden behind the large abstract painting. She pushed it. The artwork abruptly slid aside and disappeared into the wall, revealing a large safe hidden in an alcove behind it. To Piper's surprise, the large safe was old, practically an antique by modern security standards. Instead of a complex state-of-the-art computer locking system, it featured an old-fashioned number lock. Piper bit her lip and made a face.

"Shit!" she hissed angrily to herself—high-tech gadgets, she could handle easily, but this old school crap really wasn't in her bag of tricks. She lifted her wrist up to her lips and spoke quietly into a charm bracelet she was wearing that contained a hidden two-way microphone.

Down at the pool, Rocky heard the message via his invisible nano-sized spy earpiece. "Rocky," she whispered, "get your ass up here —asap. The safe has a fucking antique number lock."

Hearing this news, Rocky's merry expression dipped momentarily, but he quickly covered it up, hiding it from Torex who was looking over Michael's shoulder as he examined one of his broken toy drones.

"I'd be delighted if you could help us, Professor Braungart. I'd love to film the fireworks tonight with them."

Michael stared at the drone in his hands, bewildered—like a man trying to read instructions for a video game written in Japanese. He wanted to make an excuse, but Rocky jumped in before he could open his mouth.

"I'm sure Michael can help you," Rocky blurted out. "Meanwhile, I'd be super delighted to use your bathroom. I had a lot of *Brazil Intenso Brut* last night. That fruity and extra bubbling wine was as solid as always. It's too sad that we humans can only serve as the middle-man between the fresh and friendly fine wine in the bottle and—"

Torex raised his hand indicating "Enough—I got it." He turned and signalled Bruno, the diminutive head of his security detail. "Bruno, will you be so kind as to accompany Mr. Plouff to the bathroom?"

Bruno nodded and started walking towards the mansion. Rocky followed behind him.

"When I'm back," Rocky shouted over his shoulder

at Michael and Torex, "I wanna see some flying action here."

Torex gave him a big thumbs up. Looking a bit helpless, Michael turned his attention back to the collection of drones. He looked them over for a few moments, then shrugged.

"Well," Michael said, "we could press the start buttons again and see what happens."

"Why not?" Torex replied.

Michael went over to the drones and pressed the start buttons on several of the remote controls, but nothing moved or took off. "That's rather odd," said Michael, puzzled.

"I know. It's like shooting with blanks. It makes no sense…"

Inside the main house, Rocky trailed the pint-sized Bruno as he led him down a flight of stairs and into a hallway.

"I know what you're thinking," Bruno suddenly said.

"You do?" Rocky replied, surprised.

"You're thinking, what business does this little man have being the head of security, if he cannot even reach the top of the fridge, where all the good ice cream is."

"No, no!" Rocky insisted, "that's *so not* was I was thinking at all, brother. You know, I like to keep a low profile, even in my head. I was thinking nothing. Keeps you cool and stress-free. You should try it sometime."

Bruno let out a snort and gave him a doubtful glare. He stopped in front of a door and pointed at it, indicating that this was the bathroom.

"I'll wait for you here. Go handle your business," Bruno said in a charmless voice.

"That's really first-class bathroom decorum. Thanks!" Rocky replied with a grin. He started to head into the bathroom, then he stopped abruptly and turned around. "By the way, I hate to break it to you," Rocky said, sheepishly, "but I'm a loud person, and I'm not only going to pee in there. Now, this means two things: A) it will be noisy and B) most importantly, it will smell like hell. When I'm so close to the equator, I somehow process food like a skunk. Since we are bothers in spirit, I just wanted to let you know."

"I'll be fine," Bruno replied, looking a bit annoyed.

"Okie-dokie. But whatever happens, don't take it personally," Rocky said with a wink. "I'll see you, when I see you." Rocky then headed into the bathroom.

Bruno watched him go and shook his head,

muttering to himself in Portuguese: "Idiot."

Once he was inside the bathroom, Rocky got right to work. He reached into his shorts and took out his iPhone and a small plastic bottle filled with a greenish liquid. He went over to the toilet and placed his iPhone down on the lid of the seat. He quickly scrawled through his apps until he found the one, he was searching for, and pushed a button. Instantly, a pre-recorded audio clip of his own voice, moaning and groaning as if he was trying to pass a bowling ball through his rectum started to play. Rocky turned the volume up all the way.

Outside, in the hallway, Bruno heard the terrible noises and shook his head again.

"I'm O.K.," Rocky called out from inside the bathroom, "just getting started. Just don't interrupt me during the next couple of minutes, I gotta concentrate."

"Caramba..." Bruno grumbled.

Back inside the bathroom, Rocky eyed the small plastic bottle filled with the greenish liquid. At Rocky's direction, Michael had prepared this potent item for him using various chemicals he'd scrounged together from a janitor's closet back at the Arts & Gardens Hotel in Rio.

"Let's see what you mixed, Professor Braungart," Rocky said with a mischievous chuckle. His mirth quickly faded, however, as he opened the bottle and was instantly appalled by the terrible stench coming from the bottle. "Ohh, ohh, ohh, that's nasty!" Rocky said as he covered his nose and repressed his gag reflex. He poured the extremely smelly potion onto the floor. "Ohh, Jesus, no!" he shouted out loudly. Rocky then walked across the bathroom to a window and quietly opened it. "You gotta be strong now, Bruno. I don't want to gross you out, but my ass is going off like a freaking firehose in here, bro!"

In the hallway outside, the horrible reek from Michael's concoction wafted out of the bathroom and hit Bruno's nose. Hard. He immediately made a disgusted face like he had just stumbled upon a week-old rhino carcass.

"Puta merda!" Bruno exclaimed as he waved his hand in front of his face, trying futilely to clear the air. Just then, a couple of hot girls wearing bikinis walked by, laughing and drinking beers. Bruno tried to smile innocently as they passed, but their happy expressions instantly changed to disgust as the odor hit them. They glanced at Bruno with horrified expressions that read: *"You're really freaking gross, man!"* Bruno's face turned bright red.

"That's not me, I swear! It's the ugly American!" he insisted. His protest fell on deaf ears, however, as the hot girls hustled away to avoid the stench. Bruno covered his nose and muttered a slew of choice swear words in Portuguese.

Rocky, meanwhile, had climbed out of the bathroom window hidden behind a tree and managed to quickly scurry up the side of the villa to reach the balcony of Torex's office on the second floor without being seen. Once he had flung his bulk over the balcony railings, he quietly slipped into Torex office, joining Piper inside. Rocky smiled when he saw her and gave her a kiss.

"Hiya, boo. What's shaking?" he whispered.

"I think it's time for you to create a timely diversion so we can get this old ass safe open." Piper said.

Rocky nodded. He lifted up his arm and pressed a button on the face of his digital wristwatch. The words DRONE CONTROL appeared on the display. Beneath it another message read STATUS: INACTIVE. Rocky touched his finger to the screen, and the status changed to ACTIVATED.

At that moment, down by the pool, Michael and Torex were huddled together, examining the drones, still wondering why they wouldn't fly. Michael fiddled with the wires inside one as Torex repeatedly pushed buttons on a remote control in his hand—but nothing happened. Exasperated, Michael set the drone back down on the table.

"I'm very sorry," Michael sighed, "I don't know how to help you."

"Never mind," Torex replied jokingly. "The only thing more stubborn than these bitches is my ex!" He laughed, put part of the remote in his mouth and bit it in exaggerated comedic frustration. All of a sudden, all of the drones started to take off!

"That's it!" Michael cried with surprise. "You got it! You're a real genius!"

But Torex looked utterly petrified as he watched the dozens of drones roar into the air and buzz off in different directions.

"No, no, no!" he yelped desperately as he tried to navigate the drone storm with the one remote control he held in his hands.

Back in Torex's office, Piper kept a look out at the office door as Rocky began working on the safe. Rocky placed his digital wristwatch against the safe door. He tilted his head sideways and listened very carefully as he slowly turned the old school combination lock. Whenever he hit the right number, his watch amplified the sound of the "click" and showed the words SOUNDS RIGHT.

"How's it going?" Piper asked in a hushed voice.

"Piece o' cake...," Rocky chortled.

At the same time, at the pool, the countless flying drones had gone completely amok, causing endless havoc. The contraptions were zipping around in every direction; smashing into decorations, tearing up food buffets, dive-bombing guests, strafing angry guards who tried in vain to grab them—it was a scene of total chaos! The bikini models screamed and ran for their lives. The guard dogs went insane, barking and snapping at the drones as they whizzed by over their heads while their enraged handlers fought a losing battle to hold them back with their leashes.

For his part, Torex was still desperately trying to control the swarm of golden mini aircraft with his remote control, but his attempts to regain control only seemed to make matters worse.

"Maybe, turn it off again!" Michael shouted to him.

Torex shook the remote control violently and bit it again with his teeth—with no effect. However, a drone did start to chase after him.

"Oh, shit!" Torex cried as he ran past Michael with the flying menace hot on his tail.

Back in the hallway in front of the bathroom, Bruno waited impatiently with his thick arms crossed, still cursing to himself. Rocky's moaning and pooping sounds continued to ring out from inside the bathroom. Bruno angrily kicked a chair next to the door.

"Seriously, are you a freaking elephant? How can you still have poop left? This is ridiculous!" Bruno demanded.

"Hold on, man…," Rocky's voice on the iPhone announced. "I'm on my last inning. I'm going for my last touchdown. It's gonna be a grand..."

Hunched over Torex's safe up in his office, Rocky spoke into his watch and finished the sentence, "…finale!" With that, Rocky turned the combination lock to the final number and the safe door unlocked.

Piper sauntered up behind Rocky, smiling. "That's my boy."

He winked at her and proudly swung the safe door open. They peered inside, but a look of shock and dismay quickly spread across their faces: the safe was empty.

Rocky looked at Piper, totally baffled and pissed off.

"Damn… I hate these birthday surprises."

CHAPTER 6

Meanwhile, back at the pool, Torex's meticulously planned, fancy birthday shindig had descended into a scene of absolute mayhem as the out-of-control drones continued to wreak havoc. Michael had given up on trying to help stabilize the situation and instead had wisely decided to take refuge underneath a buffet table. He watched with considerable amusement as a pack of berserk guard dogs trying to bite darting drones, encircled a group of guards and bikini-clad models and entangled them in their leashes.

The crazed dogs suddenly charged off, dragging the entire troop across the lawn until they all crashed into the dessert table containing Torex's elaborate birthday cake. The dessert table was completely obliterated, leaving dogs, thugs and models sprawled out on the ground, covered with sticky chunks of cake and icing. One Rottweiler in particular wound up with half of Torex's cake-face stuck to its big head. Seeing this as he ran away from a robot aircraft that would not stop chasing him, Torex cried out pitifully:

"NO!!!"

This was the final straw for him. Torex decided to stop playing Mr. Nice Guy. He reached into his jacket and wiped out a semi-automatic Glock pistol. Looking backwards as he ran, Torex took careful aim at the drone pursing him. He was about to shoot it, but just before he could get his shot off, he ran right into the barrel chest of one of his lumbering henchmen and pushed the poor thug into the pool. The collision knocked the wind out of Torex. He dropped his gun and doubled over, gasping for breath.

Meanwhile, another quadcopter descended onto the second dessert table that contained several display stands filled with delectable cupcakes. The drone hovered low, then moved slowly and methodically across the dessert spread. Its propellers began striking the cupcakes, one by one, sending them flying, like bullets, in every direction. Guests and guards shrieked and ran for cover as the broadside of flying cupcakes peppered everyone, including Torex, who made the unfortunate mistake of trying to scream at someone and got a direct hit right in his open mouth.

Cowering beneath the buffet table, (using a discarded serving tray as a shield from the cupcake projectiles), Michael laughed and shook his head at the truly spectacular madness of it all.

"The only thing that would make this bash *more* perfect would be if the DJ started spinning '*Party Gone Out Of Bounds*' by the B-52s!" he quipped to himself. Just then, a large drone suddenly appeared, hovering directly in front of his face. This one was different than the others, it had little police sirens and lights on it. The helicopter made a menacing buzz as it started to slowly advance towards Michael. A threatening voice spoke to Michael, coming out of the drone's little PA system.

"Put your hands up! You've got nowhere to run!"

Michael put his hands up, but the drone didn't seem to care. It ignored his gesture of compliance and revved up its whiny motor, preparing to ram him! Thinking quickly,

Michael reached up and pulled down the tablecloth above his head, causing a large punchbowl to cascade over the side of the buffet table. Vodka infused punch from the huge bowl rained down on the bad cop drone, causing it to crash onto the lawn.

"And you've got an alcohol problem," Michael said with a smirk as he watched the drenched drone shoot out sparks, setting the alcohol (and itself) on fire. "Why do I feel, I'm in my chemistry lab?" he wondered aloud.

Across the lawn, Torex had armed himself again. He was standing on top of a table, yelling in anger, shooting drones out of the sky with his pistol. "Take that, you stupid little bastard!" he screamed as he blasted one to bits. "Who do you punks think you're fucking with?!"

Torex fired again and hit another drone, but his shot was a little off, and he only managed to wing it. The wounded drone smoked and sputtered, then fell from the sky like a doomed kamikaze, heading right for Torex!

Torex ducked the dive-bombing drone. It sailed just over his head and exploded against a large Grecian-style statue of a naked man in a boxing pose. The force of the impact caused the marble sculpture to tilt back and forth on its pedestal, then fall towards Torex. The ancient boxer's clenched stone fist hit Torex right in the crotch. Ouch!

Torex yelped, grabbed his groin area with both hands and dropped to his knees in agony.

"I hate this birthday!" he sputtered out in a high-pitched voice.

While Torex tended to his crushed tenderloins, back up in his office, Rocky was sweating bullets as he pawed around the vacant, vial-less interior of the empty safe, not knowing what the hell to do next.

"Shit! Shit! Shit!" he whispered in a panic to Piper. "If we don't find that damn vial, we're completely screwed."

"And the whole world is going down with us," Piper added.

Frustrated, Rocky banged the side of the big safe with his fist. "What kind of douche bag buys a big-ass safe and doesn't even bother to use it? I mean seriously, bro, it makes no sense!"

"You're right, babe, it makes no sense…," said Piper thoughtfully. "Torex's a whack-job, but he's not stupid. He wouldn't go to all the trouble of protecting this particular area for no reason. The virus has to be here. Which means, we must be overlooking something."

"But what?!" Rocky wondered aloud.

Just then, Bruno's enraged voice rang out again on Rocky's watchphone, cursing up a storm. Rocky spoke into his watch: "Be strong, Bruno. Think big. Stay positive, man."

Piper, meanwhile, stuck her entire head inside the huge vault and began meticulously examining it with both her eyes and her hands.

"Ah-hah!" she suddenly declared. "Son-of-a-bitch! I think I found it!"

"Show me!" Rocky said excitedly.

Piper pointed to a tiny black gap, that was almost impossible to see, on the right side of the bottom of the safe. Rocky reached into the coffer and wedged his fingernails into the small gap and gave it a little tug upwards. To his shock and surprise, the floor of the safe moved: it was a false bottom!

"Hot damn!" Rocky said as he slid the false bottom aside.

Piper shined her light in. Underneath the fake floor was a small compartment lined with foam padding. In the middle of it sat a slender vial filled with a purplish liquid.

"Well, well, well… say 'Hello' to my little friend, the T-Rex virus!" Piper said, imitating Al Pacino's Cuban gangster accent from *Scarface*. She gently plucked the vial out of the compartment and replaced it with an identical one from her pocket. She held the vial of deadly neurotoxin up for Rocky to see.

"I love you!" he gushed adoringly to Piper. "Without you, I'd just be a sorry sack of second-hand cow fertilizer, bae!"

"I know," Piper replied with a grin. She quickly secured the vial in a small, air-tight container and dropped it into one of Rocky's short's pockets. Rocky pushed a button on the face of his wristwatch.

"Whoo-hoo!" he cried out to Bruno, "it's a full house, Bruno, my-man! I'm having a great run here. Must be the climate. I'll be so done in no time."

Bruno responded with a string of angry curses, but his voice sounded garbled now, like he was very drunk or falling asleep. Rocky muted him, closed the safe and slid the colorful nightmare of a painting back to its rightful place. Then, he turned to Piper.

"C'mon, we better get the hell out of Dodge." The screaming and shooting noises from down in the pool area were getting louder and louder. "Sounds like we're missing all the fun."

"I can't believe they started the party without us!" Piper observed wryly as they went out through the balcony and began, covered from view by the tree, climbing down the side of the villa.

A few moments later, Rocky and Piper came storming out of the bathroom on the first floor, covering their noses with one hand. They found Bruno fast asleep on the ground, snoring. Rocky looked a bit surprised.

"Geez, Michael, want kinda mean knockout potion have you cooked up?"

Around the pool, the gyrocopters from hell had somehow managed to knock the portable power generator into the pool, causing a massive power surge that made all the lights, loudspeakers and other electrical equipment explode. The huge array of top-of-the-line fireworks that Torex had imported directly from China and painstakingly calibrated to lift-off precisely at 10 PM, right when he was supposed to cut his birthday cake, were now launching themselves at random. The booming pyro-techniques explosions rained showers of vibrant sparks down on the party. This, combined with the swarms of rampaging golden drones zipping around in every direction, made the whole chaotic scene looked like an epic battle out of a science fiction movie.

By this time, Michael had crawled out from underneath his makeshift bunker and was trying to fight his way towards the house, using a serving tray as a shield and the post of a sun umbrella to fight off the crazed drones. As he approached the main building, Rocky and Piper suddenly appeared at the door of the porch, taking cover from one of the mini-copters.

"Holly-molly, this is a rager!" Rocky yelled above the din of explosions, barks, screams and whizzing drones.

Just then, Piper spotted Michael on the nearby pool deck. The professor was engaged in a desperate hand-to-hand combat fight with an attacking quadcopter. Michael deflected the flying robot's charge with his serving tray, then spun around awkwardly and whacked the little beast with his improvised wooden sword, sending it tumbling into the pool.

"Hey, Skywalker, over here!" Piper called out.

Michael saw them and started battling his way across the pool deck, using his ersatz shield and umbrella pole to fend off assailing drones. After parrying off several frenzied aerial assaults, he finally made it, completely out of breath, to their side.

"Very impressed with your fancy footwork out there, Agent C2C," Rocky chirped. "You definitely got a gig waiting for you at Medieval Times if this whole save-the-world-thingy doesn't work out."

Michael pointed at the chaos unfolding all around them. "Is this one of your spy tricks?!"

A sly grin spread across Rocky's face. "A little bit. I'm a big fan of the *happiness guarantee* concept."

"Next time, do me a favour—tell me about these shenanigans before they break out. That way, I might have a vague idea what the hell is about to happen!"

"Where's the fun in that?" Rocky wondered, sounding genuinely confused.

"We'll discuss the fine points of mission prep later," Piper said. "We got bigger fish to fry, boys. Namely, that we got the damn virus, so let's bounce."

"Just leave?!" Michael said.

"Yeah, let's not spoil their party," Rocky replied just as a huge explosion echoed through the air coming from the garden, where Torex was still trying to regain control by yelling like a maniac and randomly shooting at things.

"Yes, I see your point," Michael said.

The three of them turned and quickly ran off, heading for the front gate of the villa (that was swinging from open to close and open again, since the electricity systems of the premise were going haywire). Looking through the gate made out of iron bars, however, they now saw their Fiat just going up in flames, as several misguided fireworks and a crashed quadcopter had apparently set it on fire.

"Oh, crap!" Michael cried. "Our ride's just been flambéed by your stupid drones! How the hell are we going to get out of here now?"

Rocky looked around desperately. "Quick! Find a hose, maybe we can still save it." But, just then, the Fiat's gas tank exploded—blasting the entire car to smithereens! "Or not...," Rocky groaned.

"What now?" Michael demanded.

"Now, we're totally screwed, that's what," Rocky replied dismally.

Michael gave himself a face palm.

Suddenly, Piper let out a loud laugh. "Don't cry, boys. Our plan-B is sitting right over there." Piper directed their attention to the garages next to the front gate of Torex's villa.

There clanked an open garage door that was also malfunctioning. Inside the garage, they spotted Torex's beautiful, white Maserati Gran Turismo convertible with its shiny, red interior. Piper smiled mischievously at Rocky. His face was literally glowing like a kid staring at a buttload of gifts under the tree on Christmas morning.

"Let's leave topless!" Rocky shouted. He dashed into the garage and hopped behind the wheel of the incredible sportscar.

Michael followed quickly behind him and took a seat on the passenger side, while Piper jumped into the back.

"This is so old school!" Rocky chuckled. "I know. It's mindboggling, but this car actually still responds to a key. Fortunately, I brought an all-purpose agency *can opener.*"

Rocky reached into his pocket and took out a special CIA issued fits-all-cars key. He plunged it into the ignition and immediately started the car. It roared like a mythological beast, come to life, ready to pounce.

"Me likey!" Rocky said with a wicked grin on his face.

"Please wait for me to get my seatbelt—"

But before Michael could finish his words, Rocky stomped down on the gas pedal. Michael gasped as the Maserati exploded out of the garage like a cruise missile, and they sped off into the hills as more fireworks exploded over the roof of the mansion behind them. As they roared off, two burly guards who were patrolling the area near the front gate turned to each other in astonishment.

"What the hell?!!!" exclaimed one of the thugs. "Those assholes just jacked the boss's car!"

The other guard immediately signalled two other guards standing near the villa. "Joao! Pedro!"

Quickly, the two guards rushed over to them. The four men ran into the garage, grabbed some helmets and jumped onto a pair of Ducati motorcycles. They fired up the bikes and tore out of the garage like bats out of hell, in hot pursuit of the "car thieves".

A short distance away, Rocky maneuvered the Maserati like a pro along the twisting and winding roads leading through the lush hills outside of Torex's estate. After they had travelled a few short miles, however, they suddenly heard the loud noises of motorcycles approaching them from behind. Piper turned around and saw Torex's security guards racing up on their two sleek, black Ducati motorcycles, one guard sat behind each driver, holding a sub-machine gun.

"There is a whole lot of bad asses on two motorcycles closing in!" she yelled.

Instantly, both Rocky and Piper started searching the car door's side pockets for possible weapons to fire at their chasers.

"Any weapons back there, hon?" Rocky asked.

"Just a baton!" Piper replied.

"Lovely impact weapon to bring out the good in people," Rocky said, "but a bit of a bummer when you're not a 'people person' and just want to shoot someone!"

In that moment, shots rang out—Blam! Blam! Blam!—as the guards, with the semi-automatics, started firing away at them! Rocky's side mirror exploded into shards of broken glass as a bullet ripped through it.

"Bastards!" Rocky screamed, more out of anger than alarm. "This car is a friggin' work of art! Have some respect!"

The guards didn't listen. They continued trying to strafe the vehicle with machine gun fire. Michael ducked as bullets ripped into the red leather seat behind his head, narrowly missing his cranium. Just then, one of the motorbikes zoomed up until it was right along the side of them.

The guard with the gun whipped around and pointed his weapon right at Rocky's head. He had a point-blank shot! He started to squeeze his trigger, but right before he could get his shot off, Piper hurled the baton at the Ducati's front tire. The baton hit the wheel and lodged itself in the spokes where it was instantly snapped in two with a loud crunch! Sparks flew up. The bike shuddered violently and

170

momentarily lost momentum. The guard fired, but his machine gun blast fell short as the Ducati skidded and fell behind the Maserati before the driver was able to regain control.

The guards began shooting with abandon now. Screaming hot lead filled the air. Rocky tried to avoid their incoming fire by weaving the car back and forth across the roadway. This manoeuvre worked great for a few moments as their shots all went wide, but then, Michael looked up and saw a truck moving slowly on the road directly ahead of them. Instead of slowing down, Rocky tried to zip around the rig, but as he swerved out from behind the truck, he saw another big truck coming the other direction, heading right for them!

The truck blared its horn. Impact was imminent. Now, the smart thing to do was to hit the brakes and get the hell out of the oncoming truck's path, but *Rocky* was driving. Instead of slowing down, he jerked the wheel hard to the side and steered the car towards a slopping concrete embankment rail on the edge of the road. The Maserati hit the embankment at an angle and was knocked up onto two wheels! Somehow, Rocky managed to control the car in this position and navigate it towards the narrow pathway between the two trucks.

"Hold on!" he cried. "This shit is about to get nasty!"

Michael and Piper screamed at the top of their lungs as they shot through the slender gap between the two passing trucks and came roaring out the other side, landing back on their four wheels.

Behind them, one of the motorcycles slowed and dodged the oncoming trunk, but the other one wasn't so lucky. It tried to shoot the gap like Rocky and got nipped in the rear tire. The impact knocked the bike sideways, and it skidded out. The driver and his machine gun wielding passenger were tossed from the Ducati and sent tumbling end-over-end across the road—ouch!!

The driver and the passenger on the other motorcycle whipped their heads back around and saw their fellow thugs' painful demise. This turn of events, however, seemed to only make them more determined to catch up and kill Michael, Rocky and Piper. The driver hit his throttle and raced up behind them again as his companion continued to try and rake the car with gunfire.

Michael looked worried. "Their free-bullets'-giveaway frenzy is annoying!" Michael observed dryly as he tried to find cover by ducking down.

"I love it when I get new clients!" Rocky replied as he glanced at the rear-view mirror.

"Clients?! For what?!"

"We were first-class party animals back there. We turned a run-of-the-mill terrorist b-day bash into a total banger. And when you do a great job, add value to the experience like a crazy party planer on steroids, people usually come back for more of these social events. Like these shit faces back there!" Rocky laughed.

He spun the wheel again, driving the Maserati right off the shoulder of the road and into a very bumpy patch of grass. Rocky raced over the undulating fields, then tore off through a grove of banana trees.

"This is a Maserati not a grasshopper!" Michael protested.

Rocky burst out of the banana patch and crash-landed back onto the road, barely avoiding a tourist bus. Their pursuers were undeterred, however, and stayed right on their tail, keeping up a steady stream of shooting all the while.

"I hate these heavy moments!" Michael exclaimed.

"You'll get used to bad guys trying to smoke your ass during a mission!" Piper advised, trying to calm down Michael.

"But I don't want to!"

"Well then, whiz kid, it's your lucky day today!"

"He's so adorable!" Rocky said super proudly. He smiled happily at Michael—who really looked like he was shitting his pants. "This is actually big for you. Your first seriously lethal car chase!"

"Whoopie…," Michael groaned.

They were being chased through a small beach town with a harbour filled with sailboats now. Rocky took another sharp hairpin turn and steered the car onto a wooden dock that had boats tied up either side of it. Michael peered through the windshield and saw that ahead of them the dock ended—only water stood in front of them.

"Do you know why there aren't any red traffic lights on a dock?!" Michael asked desperately and added: "Because the ocean will stop you!"

Rocky shook his head. "Unless…" He suddenly hit the brakes just as the end of the dock loomed before them. Then, he spun the wheel and made a hard righthand turn—while Michael and Piper screamed once more.

The Maserati roared off the edge of the dock and landed, not in the Atlantic Ocean as Michael anticipated, but rather, on another unseen side dock that branched out just below the main wharf.

"How the hell did you know…?" Michael wondered aloud.

"I didn't!" Rocky said, amazed by his own dumb luck. "I'm just like a charity worker. I believe in good things coming my way."

Rocky drove out of the dock area with Torex's determined motorcycled henchmen still hot on their tail. He took another sharp turn and found himself driving right down a busy street lined with tourist shops and wooden vendor stands selling fish, fruit, clothes and local tribal art. Michael's eyes went wide with alarm: the crowded thoroughfare was teeming end to end with tourists!

To Michael's absolute horror, Rocky swerved the speeding car right through the throng. Vacationers screamed in terror and scrambled in every direction to get out of the way. Rocky seemed completely oblivious to the obvious threat to life and limp as he casually veered the Maserati around darting pedestrians.

"Let's make it a shopping spree for them!" Rocky hollered as he plowed headlong through several wooden vendor stands along the street, leaving a trail of destruction and debris in his wake.

Torex's henchmen cursed loudly as they zig-zagged through the carnage, trying desperately to navigate the makeshift obstacles course. Clothes, towels, bathing suits and art, were flying everywhere—with a lot of it ending up inside the open-topped Maserati.

"Nice handbag!" Piper observed as a pretty hand-made suede purse landed in the middle of her lap.

Rocky got hit in the face by a wayward pink thong bikini that wrapped itself around his face like an octopus. Temporarily blinded, Rocky drove even more erratically, crashing through a juice stand and a fire hydrant before finally peeling the sexy bikini from his eyes.

Piper, meanwhile, saw that Michael had gotten completely buried under a pile of tourist crap. She cleared the mass and found Michael underneath with a ridiculous looking parrot bird mask stuck on his face.

A few yards behind them, Torex's thugs were struggling to keep up with the careening sportscar. In spite of their best efforts, they couldn't avoid a small heap of tourist shirts that had landed in their way. The motorcycle crashed into the mountain of tees, skidded out and came to an abrupt stop.

Seeing this in the rear-view mirror, Rocky let out a triumphant cry. He slowed the car in front of some astonished tourists taking pictures of the amazing scene on their smartphones.

"This is *so* an Instagram moment, guys." Rocky chortled. "Definitely the best mission ever!"

Rocky picked up a tribal mask (one that featured a skull wearing cool sunglasses) which had fallen on the dashboard and put it on his face. Piper snatched another one off the floor that had an image of a jaguar. Together with Michael, who was still wearing his silly-looking parrot mask, the three struck a hip pose as the "insane-animal-mask posse" for the pic snapping sightseers. Suddenly, the sounds of an angry motorcycle echoed through the air behind them again. Rocky hit the gas and drove off with their pursuers right behind them.

The Maserati roared out of the beach town and headed down a circuitous road that led into the nearby rainforest. The guard on the back of the Ducati had reloaded his machine gun and began laying down a storm of bullets in their direction again. A bullet pinged off the back of the car, dangerously close to Piper's head.

"I think our die-hard fans are getting a bit obnoxious!" Piper yelled.

"Can't you get rid of the ugly haircuts on our tail, like fast?!" Michael added.

"Yeah, totally. I'm the go-to-guy for that, bro. I'm pumped. This is gonna be popping. Watch out for the fun, kids!"

Rocky crushed the gas pedal again to get some

headway. Needless to say, he had kept on his tribal skull mask with the sunglasses. Then, he pressed a button on the dashboard which popped open the trunk lid of the car.

"Piper!" he yelled, "let's spread some summer vacation love and give these maniacs a taste of the Maserati. Send them the lid!"

"Gotcha!" Piper braced herself and started kicking the trunk lid's hinges as hard as she could, while pressing down the soft top that wanted to unfold.

"This is dangerous thinking!" Michael gasped.

"You make it sound so negative, professor!" Piper continued hammering away on the hinges with her muscular legs until the lid finally broke loose and shot with the airstream onto the motorcycle behind them.

The cover hit the front of the bike with a resounding clang! The impact knocked the driver's hands off the handlebars.

The speeding Ducati immediately lost control. It swerved off the road and crashed into the dense jungle where it bounced off several large trees like a pinball hitting bumpers, then tumbled down a steep hillside. Torex's henchmen flew off the bike and plummeted through the air, screaming their fool heads off, before making a hard landing on a canopy of tree branches. They lay there on the tree limps, groaning pitifully, as a crowd of forest monkeys gathered around them, making weird howls that sounded like laughter.

"Woohoo!" I like that!" Rocky shouted. He high-fived first Piper and then Michael, who responded a little reluctantly.

"Yeah! What an achievement, talking-ugly-sun-glassed skull face!"

"Almost too amazing for words, or to hashtag on social media. That's why you have to live through these crazy moments yourself, bro!"

"Wow, words of wisdom on top of everything else."

"Glad, you liked our little stunt!" With a sigh, Rocky finally took off his beloved skull mask and threw it away: "I think, it brought out a lovely color in me. I miss it already."

Michael took a deep breath and tried to calm himself as Rocky kept chasing down the road at insane speeds. Glancing in the rear-view mirror, Michael suddenly noticed a small, ultra-light airplane coming up quickly, at an extremely low altitude directly behind them. Instantly, his heart started beating wildly again. He tapped Rocky on the shoulder and pointed at the approaching plane.

"Uhh, Rocky, I think we might have another

problem here."

"Don't worry, bro," Rocky said with his usual cock-iness, "got it covered."

"Every time you say that, something bad happens."

"Little correction for you there, partner. I think what you meant to say was; 'something *rad* always happens.'"

"No, absolutely not," Michael insisted. "I meant 'bad' with a capitol 'B'."

The three watched as the ultra-light aircraft quickly caught up with them and moved into a hovering position directly over their heads, reducing its speed to match the velocity of the speeding Maserati. A door on the side of the tiny cockpit suddenly opened up.

"Holy shit!" Michael cried with alarm. "I think they're going to drop a freaking bomb on us!" Michael covered his head.

Just then, something did drop from the ultra-light. It fell from the sky, unravelling as it went and stopped just above their heads: *it was a rope ladde*r. Rocky let out a huge belly laugh.

"Look out below!" Rocky chortled.

Totally confused, Michael looked up and saw that Marcos was piloting the ultra-light! "Son of a bitch," he groused.

Piper grabbed the dangling rope ladder and hoisted herself onto it. Rocky handed her the container with the T-Rex virus.

"I'm getting tired of the world's most lethal virus sitting right here in my pocket, rubbing up against my papa Johnson. Take the vial to a safer place, cupcake!"

"Will do. See ya'll!" Piper said with a smile as she tucked away the container.

"Good luck, bae!" Rocky said as they blew kisses at each other.

Marcos pulled up and carried Piper off the car and soaring away on the rope ladder. Rocky glanced at Michael with a "I-told-you-so" smirk on his face.

"And you were saying...?"

"Okay, that was pretty *rad*," Michael admitted grudgingly.

Before long, the boys found themselves racing northward along the picturesque coastal highway that ran parallel to the gorgeous Brazilian coastline. This particular section of the thoroughfare was especially dangerous to navigate at high speed. One side of the road was bordered by a rambling rainforest, but the other side was a precipice of sheer, vertical cliffs that descended at a near vertical angle to the

Atlantic Ocean far below.

Rocky was navigating the treacherous road at over 100 MPH—which made Michael extremely nervous. In fact, in spite of his strenuous efforts to hide his apprehension, Michael was gripping his seat handle so hard his knuckles had turned not just white, but purple.

Suddenly, Rocky jammed on the breaks and sent the Maserati into an abrupt skidding to a stop in the middle of the road. Michael lunged forward in his seat, choking on his seat belt.

"Sorry, should have warned you," Rocky said.

Michael was confused. There was nothing around them, except for two donkeys tied up to a couple of palm trees on the side of the road.

"What now?!" Michael demanded, "do you wanna give these two donkeys a lift or something?"

"No, sweetheart," Rocky replied, "we are changing flight vehicles. It's a standard play in covert-ops; when leaving a mission area, create a clever subterfuge so your adversaries can't follow you."

"Ahh," said Michael catching on, "so, I'm guessing the donkeys are some type of subtle signal you two came up with?"

"Cor-recta-mundo, senhor."

"Nice. So, what's our new ride? At this point, I'm really hoping it's a minivan."

Rocky laughed and pointed at the donkeys.

"You got to be kidding me," Michael said with dismay.

"We need to go low-tech and get off the main road."

"Well, I suppose it's a safer option than letting you drive," Michael observed. He patted one of the donkeys on the neck. "And unlike a car, they won't produce carbon emissions either, maybe just a little methane gas if they fart, so that's good."

Turning back around, he saw that Rocky was now pushing the Maserati towards the edge of the cliff. "Whoa, whoa, whoa!" Michael protested. "Hold it right there, sparkie! Whatchadoin?"

"It's another tried-and-tested CIA procedure, Tiger," Rocky explained. "If possible, by all means, always pretend you had a lethal accident while escaping a criminal hideout... to be like Snow White making the bad queen believe she's dead."

"I totally get that," Michael observed, "but does the escape car have to fake-die, too?"

"Of course," Rocky said, gesturing at the Maserati, "that's what is called 'evidence', or do you think Torex and

183

his crew will interrogate the sharks in the sea down there to find out whether they ate us or not?!"

Michael shook his head. "See, that's where the problem of your so-far bad plan is: the car, once dumped into the sea, will cause the 47 species of sharks in the Atlantic to get sick due to it being toxic waste."

An annoyed look flashed across Rocky's face. "Tell me you're just kidding and not going full Greenpeace on me here."

"Nope, not kidding," Michael replied.

"Why not?!" Rocky exploded.

Michael took a deep breath and put his arm around his brother, trying to settle him down. "Look, I know these cliffs are a great place to start faking a deadly surprise accident. But we are *not* dumping that transport contraption with its hazardous substances into the already polluted ocean. What kind of a vacation package is that?"

"What are you saying?" Rocky growled. "Are you seriously suggesting we should detoxify the fucking car first?"

"Why does everything have to immediately start with the word 'fucking' whenever your barely interconnected neurons cannot see the big picture?! Of course, we have to do our best to detoxify the vehicle!"

"UGH!!!!" Rocky roared. "You're so beyond insane! You wanna know why I'm about this close to sending
your ass over the cliff with the Maserati?!"

"No. Tell me."

"'Cause detoxifying that sportscar is simply beyond
my current skill set!"

"Come on!" said Michael in a soothing voice. *"'If
you can dream it, you can do it.'* That's what Walt Disney
said."

Rocky stared at him, dumbfounded. "Huh?!"

"Since we are not planning on building a first-class
amusement park here or trying to conduct Mozart's Jupiter
Symphony in C major, this shouldn't be that hard. We just
need to take care of the most lethal toxic elements."

"How long is that gonna friggin' take?!" Rocky demanded. "We're kinda in a rush here, bro, you know, with
a ruthless international terrorist and his army of blood-
thirsty thugs probably hot on our trail by now, because we
professionally stole and wrecked the family's Maserati and
sent two of their henchmen hanging around in the jungle
with the monkeys. Gangsters do take these things personally, like soccer moms."

"It won't take very long, especially if you quit moaning and groaning about it. I know this seems like a needless

pain-in-the-ass thing to do, but this is precisely what C2C is all about; putting in a little time and effort to make the planet a cleaner, more liveable place. If I recall correctly, you were the one who wanted to be my co-captain leading this important movement. Does that stupid pink elephant balloon flying over your house really stand for something, or is it just another crass corporate symbol filled with hot air?"

Rocky exhaled loudly, he bit his lip—Michael was right.

"Lead the way, partner," he grumbled.

Michael patted him on the back. "That's the sprit, bro!"

At Michael's direction, Rocky soon found himself crouched on his knees, sucking hard on the end of a rubber hose as he siphoned out the gas from the car's tank into a container.

"Cannot believe, I'm actually doing this," he muttered.

"This is what living a dream is all about," Michael's voice sounded out from somewhere underneath the car. He was draining the car's motor oil into rusty coffee cans he'd found lying around on the side of the road.

"No, this is the dumbest escape routine ever." The last of the gas finally emptied into the container. "We are done," Rocky declared, but Michael poked his oil-smudged face out from under the car and shook his head. Rocky groaned.

A short time later, they had removed off all four tires from the Maserati and loaded them onto the donkeys.

"On my next escape," Rocky griped, "the first I'll do is to make sure: that you are not with me!"

"In case you were wondering," Michael answered back, "these end-of-life tires can be harvested for black carbon and then turned into powder coatings, an eco-premium product generating almost no waste."

"Oh, yeah?!" Rocky bellowed. "No waste? Your plan has just wasted 44 minutes of our precious escape time. Besides, how are we gonna get the car off the cliff now, genius?" He gestured at the Maserati, which was now sitting in the middle of the road, stranded on its axles. "By cutting off the edge of the cliff with a tasty combination of fucking cucumbers and organic toast?!"

Michael flashed a sly grin. "With this! Chewing gum!" He took out a piece of chewing gum from one of his pockets and held it out in his hand.

Rocky stared at him. His rage was about to boil

over. "Like chewing our troubles and weird insecurities away so that we can blow the car off the ground in our imagination?!"

"Yes, actually. You seemed to have forgotten that I'm an elite chemist. Thinking ahead, I prepared a couple of highly explosive chewing gums for our mission."

As Rocky looked on in wonderment, Michael strolled casually over to the container filled with gasoline that sat behind the car's rear bumper. He stuck a few pieces of his special gum around the canister, then scooped a handful of fuel out of it and poured it along the ground, making a "fuse-trail" from the vehicle over to the spot where Rocky was standing.

Michael reached into his pocket and took out a lighter. "Don't look at me like I am the first man on the moon," he said to Rocky, who was staring at him incredulously.

"I am just positively surprised."

"Great. This bang is gonna be even louder than you. So, you might want to cover your ears."

Michael bent down and lit the gas. Both of them covered their ears and watched the fire quickly race along the petrol trail until it reached the container... but nothing happened. They looked at each other and waited a few more seconds—still nothing. Disappointed, they finally lowered their hands.

"Why am I not surprised?!" Rocky said, shaking his head.

Instantly, a super loud bang went up as the gas container and chewing gum suddenly exploded! A huge fire ball shot up into the air as the car was literally lifted off the ground and hurled off the cliff.

"Holy shit!!" Rocky cried out in astonishment.

At that moment, on the sea, far below them, a young, cocky, millennial American tourist sat on a rented kayak, sipping a Brahma beer while talking to his worried girlfriend in New York via his smartphone.

"I don't know what that bang was, honey. Probably just some car backfiring or something. Don't worry, Brazil is one big non-stop party, nothing dangerous ever happens here."

Just then, the Maserati came careening out of the sky and crashed into the sea right next to the kayak with a terrific splash! The impact sent up huge waves that completely swamped the little boat, causing it to capsize. The millennial came up to the surface, moments later, clutching his phone. His panicked girlfriend's voice was screaming on the mobile's speaker.

"Oh, my God! Kenny!! Are you O.K.?! What just happened??"

"I don't know," he sputtered, spitting out sea water. "I almost just got hit by a freaking car!!"

"I thought you were kayak fishing?!!"

"I am—it was a *flying* car!"

There was a pause on the other end of the phone.

"Are you dropping shrooms again?! God dammit, Kenny! You promised me you'd lay off that shit!"

"Babe, I swear…"

Thirty minutes later, on a secluded path that wound its way through the rambling Brazilian countryside, Michael and Rocky found themselves plodding along, side by side, on their donkeys. The tires were, of course, with them. Rocky was still more than just a little peeved about the mistimed detonation.

"I just wish we still had that lovely ringing from the explosion in our ears, 'cause then I could continue yelling at you."

"Nothing lasts forever," Michael quipped. "That's why life revolves around pursuits."

"I, we, this, I...," Rocky muttered angrily, unable to

make a coherent sentence in his rage. He decided to give up on his retort and tried to calm himself by taking a few deep breaths.

Seeing his frustration, Michael reached into his pocket, took out a piece of chewing gum and offered it to him. Rocky stared at him like he was insane.

"What?!" Rocky exclaimed. "Now you want me to blow myself up?! No thanks, bro, I already feel bombed out of my mind enough for today."

"Stop worrying like a German," Michael replied with a sly grin. "That's a healthy, organic certified, 100% natural mint gum."

Rocky shook his head and took the piece. He popped it into his mouth and started furiously chewing it, like an angry dog munching on a steak bone. After a few seconds, however, Rocky's temper seemed to magically disappear. He started to smile, then laugh, harder and harder. He glanced over at Michael.

"Did you… you son of a bitch ..." It was hard for him to get his words to come out because he was chuckling so hard.

"Yes," Michael confirmed, "I spiked the gum. I just knew that at some point during this mission, you'd become pissed at me and turn into a royal pain in the ass. So, I put a lot of happy brain chemicals in the gum. 'Cause belly laughing is the best pain medicine."

Unwillingly, Rocky continued laughing. "You're so gonna pay for this! When's this gonna stop?"

A merry smile spread across Michael's face. "Sometime tomorrow…"

Back at Torex's estate, Bruno let out a huge yawn as his eyes fluttered open. He looked around for a moment, wide-eyed, disoriented, before realizing that he was lying on the hallway floor in front of the guest bathroom. Bruno slowly stood up and shook the cobwebs loose from his head.

"What the hell?" he muttered to himself angrily. "Either I passed out from that bastard's stench, or…." A look of deep concern washed over Bruno's face. He quickly scurried into the bathroom, holding his nose and noted the empty toilet seat.

He hustled out of the restroom and ran outside, checking the premises. His first stop was the garden—which he was shocked to find a total mess. Bikini-clad models and guards were staggering around in a collective daze, like combat veterans who'd just survived a horrific battle. Small fires were still smoldering here and there. Tables were overturned, the pool was littered with drones and other debris, all Torex's fancy birthday decorations were demolished, food was splattered everywhere across the patio and lawn. The drone fleet had finally been neutralized by the guards, and some of the staff were already trying to clean up the gargantuan mess in preparation for the big auction tomorrow.

Suddenly, Bruno heard gunshots ring out. He whipped his head around and saw Torex. His boss was standing in front of his ruined birthday cake, cursing as he repeatedly shot a wounded drone that was sputtering on the ground.

"Die! Die! Die! You flying imp from hell!!"

Bruno gently tapped Torex on the shoulder. "I think it's dead already, boss."

Torex gave Bruno an angry glare, then shot the drone a few more times just to be sure. "Where have you been?!" Torex demanded.

"Sorry, boss, I don't know what the hell happened. One minute I was keeping an eye on that busy American in the toilet, then I passed out."

"Passed out? Are you drunk?!"

"Of course not! I must have been drugged."

Torex was shocked by this revelation.

Bruno looked around the garden. "We need to find

that weird-looking Braungart fellow and those other two idiots who were with him."

"Michael was helping me with these stupid, fucking drones before those little bastards went totally haywire," Torex replied. "But I lost track of him in the heat of battle."

Bruno didn't like the sound of that.

Just then, an excited security guard ran up to them. "Sir," the guard said breathlessly, "that shaggy-haired professor dude and the weird Americans just stole your Maserati!"

"What?!!" Torex roared.

The guard pointed at the front gate. "Their crappy Fiat is burning in front of the house. The garage was wide open, so apparently, they just went in and helped themselves to your car. Cisco, Juan, Joao and Pedro are missing, too. They're not answering their phones. We think they took off after them."

Torex and Bruno looked at each other, confused. "Perhaps, the professor was injured and needed to go to the hospital," Torex wondered aloud. "I can't imagine a man of his sensibility and international renown needing to steal my car."

"Or maybe," Bruno replied quietly, "he stole the virus."

194

"Braungart a spy?!" Torex scoffed. "Don't be ridiculous, the man's a world-famous scientist, an environmental leader. I deeply respect him. But seriously, I mean, you saw him—does he look like James Bond to you?!!"

"Well, he is the *Sexiest Man Alive*," Bruno observed dryly. "I wouldn't trust anyone right now, boss, not even those men who supposedly took off after them. It's possible they might have stolen the virus so they could sell it off to one of your rivals themselves."

Torex paused for a moment, he suddenly looked concerned. "Go check the safe."

"On it!" Bruno replied.

He hustled back to the house. Once inside, Bruno made his way quickly to the second floor and the hallway that lead to Torex's private office. There, he found his security man lying unconscious on the floor.

"Shit!" he hissed in Portuguese. Bruno stepped over the sprawled guard and quickly disabled the laser array protecting the hallway with a remote control he kept in his pocket. He rushed up to the door of Torex's office and unlocked it with a special key. Anxiously, sweating like pig, he entered the sparse office and looked around: at first glance, everything appeared to be normal.

Bruno immediately went over to the abstract

painting hanging on the wall behind Torex's desk and slid the colorful picture aside to reveal the safe. Just then, the walkie talkie affixed to his belt crackled to life.

It was Torex. "Talk to me," Torex demanded.

"Just a moment, I'm opening the safe right now."

Bruno turned the safe's dial quickly back and forth. The lock mechanism clicked into place. Hastily, Bruno swung the safe door open, moved the secret bottom panel out of the way and peered down into the hidden compartment. A smile of relief spread across the henchman's grizzled mug: the vial containing the purplish colored T-Rex liquid was still nestled in its resting place. (This was, of course, only the phony decoy that Piper had left behind, but to Bruno's beady eyes it looked totally legit.) "Yes, it's here, boss."

"Hell, yeah!" Torex cried. "Not that I was ever worried!" he added with a chuckle.

The next day, bright and early, dozens of cars filled with scary-looking men and even scarier looking bodyguards began descending upon Torex's estate. The arriving guests were a veritable *who's-who* of the world's most notorious international gangsters and terrorists—each one was a special invitee to Torex's secret "auction".

For his part, Torex was still at a loss to explain why the hallway guard (who couldn't remember a thing except a vague recollection of chatting about Santa with "Hug-All" girl before passing out) and Bruno had fallen unconscious. Torex was troubled by this, but he reasoned that it was a *super* crazy party, so it was possible that a wayward drone had hit a pipe and started a gas leak—though, none had been discovered, yet. He had sent some henchmen out to find his stolen Maserati, but there was no time to dwell on matters as all his criminal homies were now gathering in the villa. There would be time enough to sort these mysteries out, but right now it was showtime!

The cadre of terrorists and gangsters were ushered by Torex's staff into the mansion's huge living room where they were served drinks and fancy hors d'oeuvres. Torex entered the room shortly afterwards, strutting about like a rock star, sharing ad-lib greetings with his fearsome guests. Torex took up a position at the front of the room, with Bruno at his side, holding a steel-lined briefcase.

"Friends and colleagues, I'm so glad you could join me today. We have important business to discuss. I know many of you came a long way to be here and are exceedingly busy with your various endeavors, so I'm going to cut right to the chase. You came here today for one reason—

and it's not to wish me a happy birthday. Oh, and by the way, don't ever mention my birthday to me, because my party yesterday totally fucking sucked."

Chuckles went around the room, but Torex looked deadly serious. "That's not a goddamn joke. Don't ever speak of it. Ever!"

The laughter instantly stopped.

"Anyway, moving along," Torex continued, "you came here for a very special purpose; to participate in the most important auction in human history. To bid for the right to own this..."

Torex gestured to Bruno. The henchman opened up the steel briefcase and held it aloft for all to see: inside was the vial filled with the purplish liquid.

"Behold!" Torex announced, "the most lethal substance on the planet, the one and only T-Rex virus!"

All the guests stared at the phial of T-Rex, mesmerized by the glimmering fluid inside, looking both excited by the possibility of owning the deadliest substance on Earth and slightly terrified to be in the same room with it. Torex reached into the briefcase and removed the vial. He held it carefully in his right hand and peered admiringly at the colorful fluid sloshing around inside the vessel.

"Beautiful isn't it? And yet, so dangerous. Indeed,

my friends, if one drop of the liquid contained in this vial were to be exposed to the open air, we'd all be dead in less than five seconds—and that's faster than most of you can think. Ooopps..."

On cue, Torex suddenly let the flask slip from his fingers. The criminal horde let out a collective gasp and instinctively jumped back, but Torex casually caught the container with his left hand before it hit the floor. He let out a hearty laugh.

"What the hell, Torex?!" A Russian mobster protested. "Don't fuck with us like that!"

"Relax. I'm just proving a point; just like the existence of taxes proves that you can avoid them annually and profitably," Torex said calmly.

"What point are you proving exactly? That you're insane?!!" bellowed Rafi, an agitated Malayan smuggler-king.

"No, what I just demonstrated is that T-Rex is so much more than just a lethal virus. It's also highly dangerous. What this vial, therefore, truly contains is mental *power*. The kind of power that can move things, not just people, but entire nations. Look at what I just did, to you, my friends; the smartest, most dangerous, ruthless collection of individuals on the planet. You, who fear nothing and no one, fear this. All I had to do was wiggle my little fingers and you jumped. I manipulated you. That's what T-Rex does—it allows one to set an agenda. The question is what's on that agenda, other than having our cars waxed every week. For me, the answer is very simple, and that answer is *green* …"

"Green? You mean like in money, right?" asked the leader of the biggest south American drug cartel.

Torex shook his head. "No, I mean green as in the *environment*." Torex paused and surveyed the puzzled faces of his bewildered acquaintances. "As in: saving the rainforests, echo-friendly cars and cities, clean air, unpolluted rivers and oceans, saving the planet from global warming, etc., etc. In case you haven't noticed, the world is literally on the brink of environmental destruction right now, and if we don't do something ASAP, there won't be a livable planet for us to stand on much longer—just a dust filled wasteland like Mars!"

Torex held up the bottle of T-Rex again. "But this little bit of fluid is the game-changer that can fix all that. Using this as a threat, we can force every government on Earth to sign onto to our environmental policy agenda and commit to a real, faster action plan to stop climate change and pollution overall. We can make the rules from now on.

No more of these wimpy-ass 'summits' that let govern-ments and corporations off the hook—before they even know it—with non-binding resolution bullshit, that no one ever reads. The only way to save this dying world is by making the world an offer it can't refuse; do what we say on the environment, or we release T-Rex and wipe out your whole fucking population, minus the ones that are working astronauts in outer space!"

Murmurs of shock went through the room. A screen lowered behind Torex as Bruno started a power point presentation that outlined Torex's main talking points.

"We'll start with the mandatory, highly accelerated elimination of all carbon emissions effective immediately," Torex continued. "Among the billions of cars, planes and ships, we'll make sure, the share that runs on electricity or on bio-fuel or hydrogen will grow like crazy—wilder than Banana Paul's hair. Coal plants completely outlawed. My lungs don't need them to stay healthy or free of particulate matter. Only solar and wind power will be allowed. Period. Nuclear, we'll make safe, in case we need it to like transi-tion to hot star power fusion."

"What does Jazz fusion music have to do with all this? You wanna do a hippie festival with celebrities?"

"I'm not talking music, you idiot. Fusion is down-to-earth rocket science, like bringing two nuclei of hydrogen atoms together. Bam! Lots of energy without waste!"

"Have you been reading books lately, Torex?!" One terrorist asked in shock. "You know what that can do to your brain: You read, you learn stuff, you start thinking, you start asking questions and develop a conscience. Or worse, you wanna start sharing thoughts with others and put up a freaking website or twitter your ass off. When did we gangsters ever really need that?!"

"Never, until now! It will even get better: We'll get involved in educating girls, promote inventing smart, super flexible grids and storage devices on a large scale for energy. We'll take the climate-destroying shit out of refrigeration, buy up the tropical forests to protect them. We'll reduce food waste and go meat-free like elephants, horses or bunnies do, eat lots of bendy vegetables, grill'em, put'em between slices of bread and call it a veggie burger. I know, some of you would rather swallow an earthquake. But it's time to get serious, fellas. We'll even start composting our bio-degradable leftovers, make microbes our new best friends and put real action and party back into our dead soils. All of us. No exceptions. Plus, our oceans have absorbed half of the CO_2 and lots of heat. My 4-year-old daughter and I googled some pretty great ideas as to how to get the fun back into our seas. Politicians identify their hand wave or cheesy smiles as areas for improvement, I say, the whole planet needs a makeover. Contributing to mass species extinction will become a world-wide capital offense punishable by death or two whole years of community service like planting trees."

A cry of panic echoed through the crowd of super villains when they heard the words "community service".

But Torex did not pay attention to the emotional turmoil and existential stress he was putting his homies through. Undeterred he went on: "Those nations, corporations and individuals caught engaging in anti-planet acts such as deforestation, dumping pollution into the oceans and rivers will have to answer directly to us—and not just by phone or via email. No, no, no! The days of nice little slap-on-the wrists penalties are over. You dump toxic sludge into a pristine lake, and we'll T-Rex your ass and then liquidate all your assets and split the bounty amongst ourselves. We will be the enforcers of this *New Purple Deal*."

Torex paused and let his eco-friendly words sink in, before he continued: "Why us, you ask? Because even outlaws need a healthy planet to live on. If we don't act, now, we'll all be super unhappy or dead soon—just like everyone else. You, my friends, are the alpha dogs living in the shadows of humanity and… its last hope. We are literally the toughest, most ruthless bastards in the whole damn jungle. It's up to us to save Earth because only we have the balls to do what it takes!"

As Torex finished his impassioned speech, angry, skeptical voices cried out from all over the room.

"This is bullshit?!!"

"You're a nut job!"

"What a freaking moron!"

"Are you going all Robin-fucking-Hood now?!"

"Not interested in larger-than-life volunteer work!"

"How am I supposed to explain that to my mother, huh?"

"This is too painful, Torex. What next, do you want us to also switch to light mayo?"

"We're gangsters, for Christ's sake! We don't *change* things, except our fake passports or girlfriends— may our wives never truly find out!"

Torex waved his hands in the air, trying to settle his cohorts down. "Hey, guys, people —I know, swearing is caring in our circles, but, please, chill out for a sec! How long have I known you all?" He gestured around the room at several prominent gangsters. "You, King Snake, or you,

Shot Gun, we all go way back in crime. We're family. Okay, on occasion, we shoot at each other over some minor dispute, but other than that, we are a normal family with a lot of guns, drugs, bombs and children. Now, we as proud parents want to pass on our tradition—even if your son, Tiger Shark, became one of the best hairdressers in South America. Our tradition as outlaws is at risk, our children— God bless—are at risk, because governments are not doing enough to end pollution or its equally fun-free twin, the climate crisis, that humans have cooked up for themselves. This climate-change thing is turning into a real freak-out. If the shit comes down hard, our children or grandchildren will be called Dead Snake, Tiger Shark Fin Soup, Sun-dried Shot Gun!"

Torex's passionate words were having an effect on the assembled criminals. On the screen behind Torex, numbers and graphs appeared showing the devastating effects that global warming had, not only on normal people, but also how it led directly to a sharp decline in overall criminal profits. Some of the outlaws nodded in agreement, many even started booing.

"You're fucking right, Torex! That sucks!"

"What kinda messed-up shit is that?!"

"My pizza chain is paying taxes up the wazoo!"

cried Fat Tony, a mafia boss from New Jersey. "And you're telling me the governments on this planet are calling it quits?"

Torex shook his head in disgust. "I feel your pain, Fat Tony, but what's happening here is definitely more than just a health code violation in the joints you use as fronts to sling dope—it means the end of all your customers and your profits and your kids!"

Fat Tony got even more furious. "The Brazilian nut job's gotta point here, boys. This global warming shit is worse than putting rat poison in your own friggin' sandwich!"

"It's like sticking a gun to your head and doing a hit job on yourself because you're too stupid to know no better!" another gangster chimed in.

"I hear you! I hear you!" Torex cried.

The leader of Brazil's biggest criminal gang jumped to his feet and fired his semi-automatic weapon into the ceiling.

"Good point, Big Pistol!" Torex shouted. "I'm pissed off, too, which means I'm pretty emotional right now. So, to protect our children and our evil tradition— God bless—I say, we use this lethal virus to blackmail all those freaking governments into kicking ass with the climate mess!"

"Yeah! Yeah!" the outlaws all cried in unison.

Torex raised a triumphant fist. "I say, we'll show them what real criminals can do!"

The gangsters shouted out even louder: "Yeah! Yeah!"

"Let's show'em some mad love!" Torex hollered. "Instead of bagging corrupt, but consistently incompetent officials on our pay role, I say: we'll use them to save the world! We will, starting today, form the T-Rex Network Alliance! An organization that will use all its evil, mean, ruthless mojo to get the governments of the world to do some serious good for our kids and to donate money to us, which we will accept!"

The entire room stood up and applauded, shouting out things like: "Yeah! Let's break some kneecaps for the future of civilization!"

"This is confusing, but let's do good crime for a change!"

Suddenly, there was a loud crash as Special Ops commandos, dressed in black body armor and totting compact machine guns, burst in on ropes through all the windows of the room! At that same instant, a small explosion rang out as a mini-grenade blew the room's locked door wide open!

Before anyone had time to react, dozens of commandos poured in through the breach, aiming machine guns at all the gangsters and terrorists. Everyone had the red dot of a laser site pointed at their forehead or chest. The entire room was covered. Shocked outlaws and their bodyguards, some of whom had managed to half-drawn their own weapons, immediately froze.

"HANDS UP! GET DOWN ON YOUR KNEES. NOW!" demanded the Leader of the combined Brazilian and U.S. Special Forces assault team. "YOU'RE UNDER ARREST!"

The flabbergasted gangsters and terrorists all looked around and quickly realized that they had no chance of shooting their way out of the situation.

"You gotta be fucking kidding me," muttered Fat Tony as he took his big chubby fingers off the handle of his gun and began to slowly get down on his knees.

The other outlaws cursed and began to do the same. There was one person in the room, however, who wasn't going to give up so easily. Torex raised his right hand, showing everyone, he was still holding the vial filled with the T-Rex virus.

"Don't touch me!!" he cried. "This vial contains the

T-Rex virus! Take a good look! The color purple is not your friend today! So, drop all your guns, or every one of you sons of bitches dies!!"

"No, Torex! Don't!" pleaded Big Papa, but Torex ignored his cries.

"I said, drop your weapons! I'm not bluffing!"

The Leader of the Special Ops team didn't flinch, however. "Put this brick in cuffs!" he shouted to his men.

Commandos moved in on Torex. He gritted his teeth. A wild look flashed in his beady eyes.

"Okay, you bastards, you asked for it. I'd rather die like a man, than live in a ruined world without hope! Adios, amigos!"

"NO!" Bruno screamed as Torex hurled the vial on the floor.

The vessel shattered on impact, splattering Torex and everyone else standing nearby with purplish goo. All the criminals recoiled in horror and waited with baited-breath for what they thought was an inevitable and swift death. After a few moments, however, and no one had felt like dying rapidly or falling over, they realized that nothing was happening—except them getting much closer to being arrested.

Torex looked around, confused. "W-What the hell?"

he sputtered out.

The Commando Leader laughed. "FYI, our operatives switched out the real T-Rex yesterday. What you just dropped is less poisonous than an herbal tea."

"Dammit!" Torex stammered as they put him in handcuffs, "this is even worse than my messed-up birthday!"

The Commando Leader patted him on the back. "Relax. Where you're going, you'll have lots of time for anger management classes and more…"

CHAPTER 7

PRESIDENTIAL PALACE, NORTH LEGERIA

Night had descended on the staid, but tranquil North Legeria capitol. A large thunderstorm had been forecast to arrive later that evening, and already a few raindrops had begun to fall on the monumental statues of Jimbo Jam's Grandfathers and Father which stood prominently in front of the enormous Presidential Palace.

Inside the huge mansion, Jimbo Jam, wearing Ugg slippers and fancy silk pyjamas that had his "I'm-a-hot-performer" insignia **JJ** embroidered on the back, strode down a long hallway, followed by a stoic henchman who was holding something behind his back. As he arrived at the entrance to Peggy's room, Jimbo snapped his fingers, signalling the two guards, who stood like statues on either side of the door, to give him some privacy.

The guards quickly shuffled off, and Jimbo gave the door a gentle rap. After a few moments, Peggy's voice responded from somewhere inside, she sounded a little preoccupied.

"Yes?"

"Hey, sweetie pie, it's me—your favourite OG. Just came by to say 'yo' and see how your special project was coming along. Is it done, yet?"

"Almost," Peggy answered back. "I'm just finishing up the final edits. I'm gonna upload it soon."

"Sweet!" Jimbo tried to open the door, but it was locked. "Can I come in? I'm like dying to see it."

"Sorry, baby doll, you know I'd love to give you a special preview, but that'd ruin the surprise. You wouldn't want that, would you?"

"Sure, I would. Stop being a freaking tease. As President, I order you to open this door at once!"

"Seriously, bruh? You sound just like my dad."

"I'm just kidding!" Jimbo said, rolling his eyes. "But like for reals, why can't you just cut me some slack here, yo? I thought we were *The Dream Team*." Jimbo looked at his henchman—am I right? The stoic man nodded in agreement.

"We are, boo…. It's just that, well… there's just some things a woman has to do by herself. It's gender equality thing. Sorry, you'll just have to be patient and wait for the official launch on my YouTube channel like everyone else."

"You suck," Jimbo said with a sigh. "Fine, I'll wait."

He snapped his fingers, and his stone-face henchman set the object, he was hiding behind his back, gently down on the ground in front of Peggy's door.

"By the way, I brought you a little gift. I guess I'll just leave it here outside your door. Hit me with a text if you want to hang after the premiere or something. I'll be in my room." Jimbo Jam walked away, followed by his dutiful henchman, looking very disappointed.

Needless to say, pissed-off General Takeshi, the resourceful, highly decorated head of security and lifetime member of the country's hall of the people's heroes, scoffed like a professional junkyard dog at the surveillance monitors.

What he had just witnessed happening in the hallway, in front of Peggy's door, was simply too much rocking the boat. In his sclerotic mind, he marched down memory lane, dragging the images of JJ and Peggy along, until he could find the right "consequence-to-action" idea. It was, to put it mildly, the opposite of what any good boy scout (hoping to make his parents proud) would do to his fellow humans, or what would be considered a great, legal pitch on a crowd-funding platform. In Takeshi's sick mind, however, JJ and Peggy had become the *duo infernale* which could entice the citizens of North Legeria to become too tough a crowd—simple state terror would, in the future, then no longer please them. This meant danger and also, "This cannot be good."

As Takeshi most enthusiastically thought of himself as the only smart guy in the surveillance room, he congratulated himself to his clever plan, involving parts of the bribed army loyal to him, of icing the two lovebirds—sooner rather than later. For the moment, though, Takeshi continued starring at the monitors with the life-changing footage from the hallway in front of Peggy's suite. Indeed…

…after a few moments, Peggy opened her door. She was

wearing a long, elegant Asian nightgown that Jimbo had given her. She poked her head out, looked down and her expression went from curious to warmed; lying at her feet was a beautiful, little bonsai tree in a small porcelain pot. Peggy smiled, genuinely touched by the gesture. She picked up the bonsai. When she rose again, Peggy noticed the tiny camera hidden at the ceiling. As usual, she couldn't resist, waved and smiled at the observation device. Then, seductively wiggling a little bit with her buttock, she went inside her suite and closed the door.

For the outraged, vampire-face general Takeshi in the control room, this was like Peggy had personally punched him in his face while screaming the declaration of independence at him.

In her suite—unaware that she had just caused Takeshi to release a furious avalanche of curses—Peggy walked back across her room and set the exquisite bonsai tree down on a desk next to her laptop computer. The front page of her YouTube channel was on the screen. The channel's name was *Beautiful Balanced Planet*—it had over 40 million subscribers. It featured numerous documentary shorts written and produced by Peggy on environmental subjects like: "Reforestation", "Regenerative Agriculture", "Epigenetics", "Circular Economy", "Gender Equity: A

Key Answer to Solving the Planetary Challenges".

The laptop let out a small beep, indicating that the latest video she had just edited was finished uploading. This documentary was also titled *Beautiful Balanced Planet*. Peggy moved her cursor over to the "post video" button on the screen. She hesitated for a moment, with her finger hovering over the mouse, wondering to herself if there was anything she had left out. Finally, she took a deep breath and launched her brand-new video. She watched as the video began to play.

Peggy's documentary started off with footage of street protests by young activists from all around the globe speaking to politicians and world leaders. Then, she reported about how *Greta Thunberg* had demanded climate action at the United Nations and listening to scientists.

Next, Peggy highlighted world-renowned people with suggestions for solutions: Ellen MacArthur, the successful solo long-distance yacht woman, who was also inspired by Cradle to Cradle, promoted a positive, prosperous circular economy. Pioneering fashion designers, like Stella McCartney—who was also an animal rights activist—led the way to embracing the concept of sustainability in fashion by also focusing on a circular economy that created positive impacts. Pioneers of organic farming, like Prince

Charles, raised awareness of Nature's core feature of harmony—just like Einstein had revealed it regarding the great unity of the cosmos with his theories of relativity.

Al Gore was also featured with his call for urgent action on the climate crises. Paul Hawken and, for instance, Kathrine Wilkinson from the Drawdown Project, Peggy pointed out, presented lists of the best already existing practices to overcome the global climate challenge. Arnold Schwarzenegger was known, as Peggy delineated, for his ongoing efforts to combat climate change with a positive vision on sub-national levels. In 2007, as Peggy also reported, Governor Schwarzenegger had supported the crafting of the ground-breaking *California Green Chemistry Initiative* and had signed two bills of this initiative into law on September 29, 2008. Part of the top policy recommendations was to "Move Toward A Cradle-to-Cradle Economy" as the press release of California's Environmental Protection Agency in 2008 stated. With California being the world's 5th-largest economy, this represented a comprehensive shift with respect to the regulation of the chemical industry of the United States. All this also led to Schwarzenegger's support of the launch of the *C2C Products Innovation Institute* in 2010. China as well took inspiration from the Cradle to Cradle design practice both for its

2004 *Circular Economy Initiative* and for its 2008 *Circular Economy Law*.

Finally, of course, Agent C2C, aka Michael, spoke in an interview with Peggy: "Our nutrient-rich materials," Michael explained in his clip, "using C2C concepts, can make beautiful, eco-intelligent and positive products like clothes, homes, furniture, cars, ships, trains, planes. Using existing and new innovative technologies, our amazing cities can also be precious, positive, eco-intelligent material banks: fully reusable, safe resources to build a smart, prosperous future. We just have to follow nature's law of return, the holistic concept of the nutrient cycle to end pollution—become positive by making 'waste' a nutrient—and to become climate positive both by fully reusing valuable materials and by using renewable energies. C2C 4 C, Cradle to Cradle for Climate. As I like to put it: *Our world can be fun for everybody if we do it right and see Nature as our teacher!*"

As the clip of the interview ended, the documentary cut to footage of Peggy at a huge rally in front of the marble statue of Abraham Lincoln in the National Mall in Washington D.C. Peggy was wearing a badge that said, "Beautiful Balanced Planet" on it. She shouted into a megaphone to the huge crowd:

"We will take our future back together!!"

The video stopped. Instantly, a tear ran down Peggy's cheek—even though, she had seen the video countless times during the edit, it still moved her deeply. She reached over to the small Bonsai tree sitting on her desk and touched its leaves for comfort.

On the laptop screen, the views of her new video recorded by YouTube started accumulating in real time. The view counter raced from hundreds to thousands to millions in just a matter of seconds.

Down the hallway, inside his gigantic personal suite, Jimbo Jam, sat up in his super large golden bed in in his magnificent bedroom watching the end of Peggy's video on a golden notebook computer embroiled with diamonds. His face was filled with emotion as the video came to an end.

"Way to go *Dream Team*…," he said, wiping a tear away.

At that same moment, halfway across the world, someone else was also watching the video, too. Peggy's father, President Munger, sat hunched over the Resolute desk in the Oval Office, taking it in on his personal computer. As credits rolled, he continued to stare at the screen for a long time.

The video had hit him hard. Not only because of the prescient environmental message, but because he knew that this was his lost daughter's message to him, personally. His expression read: worried, proud, regretful and committed, all at the same time.

The spell was broken by a knock at the door. President Munger looked up as his chief of staff entered the room.

"Sir, sorry to interrupt, but the U.S. Ambassador to the UN is on the line. He would like to know if you will personally attend the UN summit on climate solutions and the circular economy?"

The President nodded affirmatively. "Absolutely. We need to make this conference a top priority."

"Very good, Mr. President. I'll let him know. Also, I have wonderful news. I just spoke to CIA director, Robert Jordan. The mission in Brazil was a total success. We retrieved the T-Rex virus and rounded up Torex and countless other top terrorists. The Director will be by shortly to debrief you on all the details, sir. It looks like Torex actually wanted to use the T-Rex virus to blackmail governments to take more rapid actions on the environmental issue."

President Munger, let out a huge sigh of relief.

"Congratulations, Mr. President. I hate to admit

when I'm wrong, but it looks like, betting on Agent C2C was the right choice, sir."

For the first time in a very long while, President Munger allowed himself to smile…

A few days later, rumours swirled around Washington as details began to leak out of Michael's incredible exploits that saved the world from the deadly T-Rex virus. The media picked up on the story, and President Munger was finally forced to give a press conference addressing the crisis where he generously praised professor Braungart for his bravery and service to humanity. Social media, of course, went completely insane. The headlines of newspapers and internet articles screamed things like:

SEXIEST MAN ALIVE SAVES WORLD FROM LETHAL T-REX VIRUS TERRORIST AT- TACK!

FAMOUS CHEMISTRY PROFESSOR HUNTS DOWN TOP INTERNATIONAL CRIMINAL MINDS

LIKE JAMES BOND: CHEMIST & SEXIEST MAN ALIVE ROUNDS UP THE WORLD'S MOST WANTED!

Michael wasn't just the *sexiest man on the planet*, anymore, now—he was its biggest hero! Still, the humble professor wasn't going to let it all go to his head. In spite of his new-found celebrity status as the saviour of the planet, Michael was determined to return to his normal routine.

So, a week later, he found himself standing at the podium in the largest lecture hall at The University of California at Santa Cruz, (who's loveable mascot is, by the way, the Banana Slug). The auditorium was packed. Standing room only. On a large screen behind Michael was a picture of Albert Einstein together with a quote by him:

"The world as we have created it is a process of our thinking. It cannot be changed without changing our thinking."

"Einstein discovered that the cosmos is a harmonious whole," Michael said to the audience. "To achieve his revolutionary success, he—as the bold, freely thinking, breaking-the-mould-type genius—relied on just one, I repeat, just one most simple, purely mathematical and amazingly beautiful idea: the balanced, harmonious concept of symmetry, which physicists, starting from Galileo to Newton to most groundbreakingly Einstein, followed by mathematician Emmy Noether, and later physicists in the realm of quantum mechanics, detected in nature in a central role. Symmetry means that two—even seemingly different—phenomena are actually the same, by, e.g., doing the same thing."

For a moment, Michael paused and smiled at the audience: "By the way, if you guys think I'm exaggerating the importance of symmetry in nature, just imagine your left foot being as big as a bus and the other as small as a spider. Say, a bear comes by for lunch and jumps at you, and you want to run away with these two asymmetric, disharmoniously working feet. Let me know how well that works out for you!"

A giggle reverberated through the lecture hall.

Michael advanced the power point presentation to the next slide. On the screen, a picture appeared delineating symmetry. It showed two identically shaped, but differently colored, round spheres: one light red on the left, one blue on the right. And since they were the same, an equal sign stood between them. Michael had labelled them: Phenomenon #1 = Phenomenon #2—in reference to Einstein, who had shown that, e.g., both the phenomenon of *gravity* and the phenomenon of *acceleration* are the same, since both phenomena *do the same thing* of warping spacetime.

"As you see in this visual," Michael continued, "both these phenomena shapes are identical, both can, therefore, exchange places…"

Michael hit a button on his handheld remote, and the two spheres started moving towards the other side of the equation, where they were allowed to be placed, since both spheres were equal. The red, left sphere moved to the right above the equal sign, and the blue, right sphere advanced below the equal sign towards the left side. This caused a circular motion, since the spheres just kept moving from one side to the other. Symmetry, that made two phenomena equal via the equal sign between them, was not static, but the balanced, harmonious und all-unifying foundation of a circular and cyclic motion. The recipe of continuous transformation, the simple, all-encompassing recipe of nature.

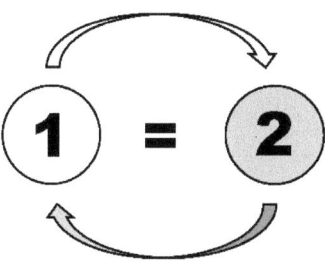

"…And that creates the concept of the circle and cyclical motion in nature, which we know as nature's nutrient cycle which ensures that **WASTE equals FOOD** or nutrients. So, `waste´ becomes nutrients or food, and that becomes `waste´ once more, which becomes nutrients again and so forth. Nothing is lost, all is intertwined, part of a dynamic, positive whole and perpetually cycled, since this unity, this whole is inherently cyclical. Accordingly, the linear model of *take-make-waste*, which our current economy is mostly based on, is dumber than aiming for the world record in head injuries. Linear makes no freaking sense! C2C-circular does!"

The audience laughed and started to applaud real loud.

Outside the lecture hall, two distinct, elderly professors walked by and heard the cheerful noise blasting through the open hallways and doors.

"Braungart is back!" one professor enlightened his bewildered colleague.

Inside the lecture hall, the good mood generated more signals of optimism and outbursts of joy among the audience.

"I LOVE YOU, MICHAEL!" someone female yelled real loud from way up in the auditorium. This was automatically accompanied by sharp whistles, countless "Woohoos!" and more cheering.

"You sound like a lot of extra fun this morning, sunshine!" Michael shouted back quickly and caused some more roaring laughter. "I love you right back other person in the audience!" Then he smiled at the happy crowd of students. "I love you, too. I love all of you. Not because I'm a super excited, super charged cheerleader. But because we need you, young people! We need the best scientists at the helm of companies to drive ahead positive innovation!!! We also need the best researchers, the best engineers, the best marketing people, the best managers, the best community workers, the best teachers and the best artists, the funniest comedians to get us back on a positive, fun track with Nature! More than ever, everyone counts these days!"

The circle of Michael's power point presentation

now morphed again to form the diagram of the C2C nutrient cycle.

"That's nature's simple, all-encompassing scheme of the cycle which the design concept of C2C is built on."

The rapt audience let out "ahhs" and nodded along—totally getting the visual concept. Michael clicked his remote again. Now, a new picture appeared on the screen, it depicted the two C2C Cycles; the CYCLE OF THE BIOSPHERE and the CYCLE OF THE TECHNOSPHERE. Both cycles displayed the same phases, highlighting how a product was first manufactured, secondly used by the consumer, eventually returned at the end of its usability and then in a next step dismantled—either by, e.g., composting it in the biosphere or by taking the ingredients apart in the technosphere.

Both the biological composting and the technical dismantling of the products resulted in so-called precious nutrients or valuable components that could be used again to create a new product either in the bio- or technosphere. Needless to say, products that were designed from the beginning to be perpetually cycled saved a lot of energy, helped to go easy on resources and allowed to keep the environment intact. This meant also saving a lot of money for businesses and making them more profitable on so many levels. So, both planet, people and profits literally got a continuous boost from either the positive effects of keeping toxic, but valuable materials safe in the technopshere or from the benefits of the nutrient-rich, organic components in the biosphere.

"Cradle to Cradle," Michael explained, "uses two identical spheres or symmetric cycles that, even though, they appear to be different spaces or realms, do the same thing of generating positive, cyclical effects for both people and planet."

Next, a chart filled the screen that presented three sets of data:

1. **55% of greenhouse gas emissions** *are caused by: producing/handling energy and using materials like in refrigeration*

2. **45% of greenhouse gas emissions** *are caused by: the way we produce/use products/goods and manage land.*

3. ***SOLUTION: a C2C-inspired circular economy*** *with biological and technical cycles that is underpinned by effective and efficient renewable energy and energy measures in general.*

(Source: Completing the Picture, report by the Ellen Mac-Arthur Foundation, 2019)

Michael gestured at the numbers.

"To successfully turn the manmade greenhouse gas problem around, which is a waste-in-the-atmosphere crisis—due to destroying the natural carbon cycles—both sectors that generate greenhouse gases have to become symmetric. They have to start doing the same thing, by both reducing the emissions and start generating positive effects for both people and planet via a C2C-based, positive circular economy—"

Just then, Michael was interrupted as his smartphone began ringing. His face turned bright red. "Sorry. I should have put my damn phone on vibrate." The audience laughed.

Michael took his phone out of his jacket pocket to turn the ringer off, but he hesitated when he glanced at the screen and saw who was calling him: *it was President Munger.* Michael sighed and looked apologetically at the crowd.

"I'm so sorry, my friends, but I have to take this. This is major world politics calling."

Michael turned away from the podium and took the call on the wings of the stage. He listened to Munger on the other end of the line for a few moments and couldn't believe what he was hearing.

"What the hell?!" he finally said in an exasperated voice...

THE WHITE HOUSE, 8 AM

As the golden rays of early morning sun shone on the stately columns of the White House, a crucial meeting was commencing inside the Oval Office. The U.S. Ambassador to the United Nations, Barry Hogan, stood in the center of the room, addressing President Munger, Robert Jordan—the CIA director—Michael, Rocky, Piper and the Secretary General of the United Nations, Aiki Saito.

"Good morning, ladies and gentlemen," Hogan began, "thank you all for coming here on such short notice. I give the floor to the United Nation's Secretary-General, Aiki Saito." Hogan sat down, and Mr. Saito walked in front of the group.

"Thank you, Mr. Ambassador," Saito said politely to Mr. Hogan. "Mr. President, hello everyone." Michael, Rocky and the others murmured ad-lib greetings. Saito continued. "Yesterday, I received this video from North Legeria's Ambassador to the UN, which the U.S. President has already seen."

A large screen that had been set up behind Saito came to life. A video began to play. Jimbo Jam appeared. He was standing in an ornate room somewhere inside his Presidential Palace, dressed in his usual bling.

"This is Jimbo Jam, North Legeria's current leader, as you all know," Saito explained.

In the video, Jimbo smiled merrily, then started speaking in his native language.

"Hello!" Said Jimbo in North Legerian.

"He just said `*Hello*'," Saito translated.

Rocky nodded in agreement. "That does make kinda sense."

Then, in the video, a person—covered head-to-toe by a black blanket—appeared, being guided into the room by two guards. They directed the mysterious person under wraps to a position next to Jimbo Jam.

"What the heck is this all about?" Michael wondered aloud.

"Just watch!" Saito replied.

With a sudden cry of "Wah-la!", Jimbo pulled down the blanket to reveal… Peggy, wearing nothing but her super-mini, sexy, red dress and red pumps! The video stopped, frozen on this frame. Everyone's collective jaw dropped.

"Peggy...," the President muttered in dismay.

Rocky patted the President on the shoulder, feeling his pain. "Wow, that's tough, bro."

Saito cleared his throat, but before he could say something, President Munger continued: "As you can see, my daughter is in North Legeria." President Munger said with a sigh. "At first, we thought she had been abducted, but now we know she went on her own free will."

"How was this possible?" Michael cried.

"Peggy said she wanted to go hiking in Thailand," President Munger sighed. "I thought that was a healthy, friendly, properly dressed idea I should support as a father."

"That doesn't look like a hiking outfit." Michael observed, eyeing Peggy's sexy, red dress.

"Peggy thinks she's got the cosmic go-ahead for everything. She never uses the stop button really. Being disruptive nonstop and thinking independently is, I guess, her strong suit."

"Yeah, like hot, motivating, red dresses," Rocky chimed in. "Next time, tell her to go hiking and climbing like *that* in Vegas. They always have half-naked—" Rocky caught himself, seeing President's Munger's pissed off reaction. "—but *classy* women from all kinds of places in their shows. I think, that might be her thing! She already has a heart-warming show reel."

Munger stared at Rocky, stone-faced, like he wanted to punch him in the nose.

"Thank you," Saito said to Rocky. "I'm sure the President will consider appointing you as the first goodwill ambassador of the UN to Las Vegas, once we have solved this international crisis."

"Always happy to help the world community!" Rocky replied giving a thumbs up.

"Right… so, moving on." Saito took out a letter from his jacket. "This game-changing letter came along with the ambitious video. It's hand-written by Jimbo Jam himself."

"Is he making crazy or creative threats again?" asked Piper.

"No, it's a unique invitation, actually," President Munger interjected, "from Peggy and Jimbo Jam."

"What does it say?" asked Michael.

"He and Peggy want you, Michael, to come to North Legeria and help them to transition the entire country to a Cradle to Cradle, circular economy. In exchange, Jimbo Jam promises to eliminate his nuclear arsenal and democratize his country."

"What?!!" Michael blurted out in astonishment.

A short time later, Michael found himself huddled with Rocky and Piper in one corner of the Oval Office while the Secretary General, Ambassador Hogan, the CIA Director and President Munger carried on an intense discussion on the other side of the room.

Michael was shaking his head emphatically. "Absolutely not! This is getting totally out of control!" he roared.

"I know," Rocky said, trying to sound sympathetic. "But on the other hand, it's a great opportunity."

Piper agreed: "I was gonna say. You could so inhabit the moment, Michael. You know, be the power of now, if you help turn Jam's autocratic country around."

"Sure," Michael replied, "but this is a highly unstable country."

"You're right," Rocky concurred. "There are probably some rogue elements of his army that he fears, and he is looking for a way out."

"But then again," said Piper thoughtfully, "if it works out in a place that extreme, all the other countries will be forced to implement Cradle to Cradle much faster, or else they'll look stupid, and Jimbo Jam will steal the show."

Rocky nodded. "Great point, hon."

Piper gave Michael a friendly kiss on the cheek. "You know, if it was me, I'd already be on that plane to North Legeria."

"That's because you're crazy, and you're Rocky's girlfriend."

"True that," Piper replied, gesturing at Rocky. "I'm stone cold in love with this dude."

Rocky blushed. His voice choked up with emotion. "Man, you guys are killing me. I mean, first that hot, almost buck-naked daughter of the President, and now you two hitting me with these love themes. This is like literally killing me softly. I'm so not prepared for this emotional shit. Guys, we *have to* group hug right now." Rocky started putting his big, meaty arms around everybody.

"Please, Rocky, don't! Not here!" Michael tried to resist, but before he could step away, Rocky had wrapped him up like an octopus.

Just then, Saito, the U.S. Ambassador Hogan and President Munger approached them.

"Uhh, guys… I hate to interrupt your tender family moment here," Saito said, sounding a bit impatient, "but time is running short. Have you made a decision, Professor Braungart?"

Everyone looked at Michael with anxious, pleading expressions etched on their faces. Michael stared back at them for a moment, trying to resist their collective will, but he knew he was fighting a lost cause. Finally, he rolled his eyes and gave them a defeated shrug.

"I trust that, at least, we'll be flying to North Legeria first class?"

CHAPTER 8

U.S. MILITARY AIRCRAFT, SKIES OVER NORTH LEGERIA, 11 AM

Michael, Rocky and Piper sat huddled together in the empty cargo space in the back of a huge C-130 Hercules transport plane. They had been issued insulated Air Force survival jackets, but they still couldn't help shivering from the intense cold.

"I should hit the call button, that stewardess is taking forever with our mimosas!" Rocky quipped, blowing into his half-frozen hands.

"I hate you, right now," Michael growled.

"Funny, bro. I know you don't mean that."

Michael glared at him. "No, trust me, I really do."

Just then, the pilot's voice came on over a crackly loudspeaker: "We are now over North Legerian territory, flying at an altitude of 25,000 feet."

"Coolio!" Rocky exclaimed. "We're almost there!" Suddenly, the plane lurched hard to one side, making an evasive maneuver, then dropped a few hundred feet. Rocky laughed hard as his stomach leapt up into his throat, and he looked like he was enjoying this, like a kid on a roller coaster. He noticed, however, that Michael looked a little green around the gills.

"You O.K., big guy?"

Michael shook his head and sucked in a deep breath. "Not really, and this has nothing to do with the fact that words like `friend´ have become a verb due to the internet."

"That's truly amazing. Also, words like `like´ are now a noun, too. Speaking of liking, what's bothering you?"

"Well, ever since I climbed that chimney back then to protest against pollution, I have a fear of heights."

"Don't worry," Piper assured him, "you're wearing a state-of-the-art survival jacket including a parachute."

"Parachute?" Michael said with surprise, indicating that he was not going to "friend" or choose the "like option" regarding the instant parachute message he had just received.

Rocky grinned at him. "Yeah, you know, in-room dinning, in-house delivery, right?"

"Yeah, sure?!" Michael replied, anxiety rising in his voice.

"Parachuting is the exact opposite of that," Piper said smiling. "It's all about jumping outside, regrouping where the fresh air is, laughing it up in the sky where the birds fly high."

"Wonderful!" Michael replied incredulously. "I'm all about outdoor activities."

"By the way, bro," Rocky inquired, "is it true that you peed into that chimney?"

In spite of his nausea, Michael couldn't help chuckling a bit at the memory. "Not only that—" Michael wasn't able to finish his thought, as at that precise moment a huge explosion rang out.

The entire plane shuddered and rattled violently, then it started to descend rapidly.

"Shit!" Rocky cried.

"What happened?!" shouted Michael in a panic.

The question was answered instantly when the pilot's unnerved voice came over the PA: "We just got hit by a surface-to-air missile... One wing is broken.... Can't control the plane anymore..."

Michael shot a look of concern at Rocky and Piper. "That sounds bad."

"It sure ain't splendid," Piper remarked.

"Looks like those rouge military elements don't want to invite us over for tea," Rocky grumbled as he and Piper snatched up helmets that were hanging on a nearby rack.

They quickly strapped their headgear on. Rocky then stuffed a helmet over Michael's shaggy head and clipped it in place. Michael just stared at him in a daze, like a deer frozen in headlights. Then, Rocky turned and hit a big metal button on the side of the fuselage with his fist. Red lights began flashing along the interior of the hull as the large rear door of the plane opened up, exposing the cargo hold to the open sky. Howling wind gusted in through the huge portal.

Michael's eyes bugged-out as he gawked in terror at the open hatchway yawning before him. Rocky grabbed him by the front of his survival jacket and started dragging him towards it.

"Let's go parachute!" he cried out to Michael above the din of the wailing wind. But Michael began clawing at Rocky's hand, trying desperately to pry himself loose from his half-brother's grip.

"What?! No!! I'd only do that in an emergency!" Michael protested.

"This is an emergency, sweetie!" Piper hollered as she helped Rocky shove him towards the door. "Evolve with the game."

"B-But... I've never used a parachute!" Michael stammered.

"Then it's even more of an emergency!" Rocky shouted.

With considerable effort, they managed to pull and shove Michael right to the end of the cargo ramp.

"Now get out!" Rocky ordered.

Michael took a quick glance down: the front of his tennis shoes hung over the edge of the floor, below them, he caught glimpses of the rolling North Legerian landscape through puffy clouds. In his terrified eyes, the mountains looked like tiny ant hills and huge lakes were the size of rain puddles; it all came across to Michael like the view one might see in a photo of Earth taken from the International Space Station.

Instinctively, Michael tried to backpedal away from the edge of the cargo ramp, shaking his head wildly from side-to-side, but Rocky and Piper had a firm hold on him and wouldn't let him retreat.

"Hell, no! This is too high!" Michael pleaded.

"What kinda excuse is that?" Rocky demanded.

He and Piper then summoned all their might and with a big heave-ho, shoved the panic-stricken Michael out the back of the plane. Michael let out an ear-piercing, high-pitched shriek (the kind of wail a teenage girl would make if she ran into a knife wielding killer in a horror movie) as he tumbled end-over-end into the wild blue yonder.

As he plummeted through the air, Michael started flapping his arms like a bird (as if that would help somehow) while continuing to scream out his mantra: "Too high!! Too high!! Too high!!!" at the top of his lungs.

Back on the rapidly descending plane, Rocky and Piper readied to make their jumps.

"This is gonna be fun and special on every level!" Piper yelled to Rocky.

He gave her a wink. They held hands and both leapt out of the plane together. At the front of the aircraft, the pilot jumped out an escape hatch behind the cockpit just before a second missile hit the aircraft, and it exploded in a huge fireball! The four skydivers fell for a few second before their chutes all opened up automatically.

After he started floating, Michael's squealing finally subsided. He took several deep breaths and looked down: beneath him there was only jungle.

"Great... Where exactly do those fools think we're supposed to land?" Michael grumbled to himself in a low voice—not realizing that his helmet was equipped with a radio transmitter.

Suddenly, he heard Rocky replying back to him over a speaker inside the headdress. "It's not so much a question of where, bro, 'cause it's definitely gonna be jungle."

"It is more a question of how?!" Piper said, finishing his thought.

A few minutes later, a troop of Gibbon apes, who were munching on fruit in the forest canopy, looked up in surprise as a strange, gangly creature floated down out of the sky and landed on some nearby branches. The weird "bird" (by their reckoning) made a lot of funny noises when it descended, chirping something that sounded like, "Ouch! Ouch!" as the tree limbs broke its fall.

They watched with amusement as it tumbled through the foliage and ended up dangling beneath a large branch, upside down. A few moments later, it was joined by a second "big, dumb bird" who also sucked at landings. Just like the first one, it plunged through the leaves and soon found itself hanging upside down beside its companion. The Gibbons just shook their heads at the two pathetic birds, feeling sorry for them before going back to eating their mangos and large papayas.

Hovering awkwardly upside down, about six feet above the ground, their faces rapidly turning purple from the blood rushing to their heads, Rocky and Michael were feeling a bit anxious to get out of their latest predicament.

Michael continued to yelp, "Ouch, ouch!"

"Your balls?" Rocky inquired.

"No, wisdom teeth," Michael replied.

"Lucky bastard," Rocky moaned as he fiddled around his waist, trying to loosen up the tight harness that was constricting his tenders. He suddenly remembered something important and looked around. "By the way, where is Piper?"

Right on cue, Piper came crashing down through the trees, head-first and came to an abrupt halt, dangling next to Michael and Rocky. She looked at them and snapped a bubble with her chewing gum.

"That's the first time I ever popped a bubble with my

head facing earth. Cool!"

Suddenly, they heard the sound of multiple cars approaching. Rocky looked off and saw a dozen off-road military vehicles came speeding towards them.

"Here come the jungle poets," he muttered.

The military convoy quickly surrounded them and screeched to a halt. A squad of elite North Legerian soldiers leapt from the cars and ran up to Rocky, Piper and Michael with guns trained on them.

"Don't expect good manners," Piper whispered to Michael. "We're not in their friend zone."

"How y'all doing?" Rocky asked in a friendly voice.

The Commander responded by whacking him upside the head with the butt of his pistol.

"Well, at least they knock," Michael noted.

From nearby trees, soldiers cut the cords of the parachutes. Piper, Rocky and Michael fell hard on the ground, landing face-first with a collective thud. The anxious commandoes shouted something hostile at them in North Legerian and sprayed the ground in front of them with a volley of machine gun fire. Michael, Rocky and Piper got the message. They raised their hands in the air and kneeled down before them.

Piper leaned over to Rocky. "Trigger-happy and nervous—not a good combo."

Rocky nodded in agreement. For the first time, he looked a little concerned as he watched the Commander continue to rant and rave at them in his native tongue.

"I don't think this is gonna end well, bro," he said to Michael.

"For them," Michael replied with a twinkle in eye.

Rocky looked at Michael, wondering what he was up to....

Suddenly, Michael then started to speak to the soldiers in perfect *North Legerian*. "I have something mind-boggling for you!" Michael said to the Commander.

The soldiers looked at each other, shocked at Michael's fluency. The angry Commander also seemed impressed that he spoke their language.

"What?!" the Commander demanded.

"It's in my right breast pocket," Michael replied casually.

The Commander marched over to Michael, reached into his right breast pocket and took out three red, spherical lollypops. He stared at them for a moment with an inscrutable expression on his face, then, suddenly, burst out laughing. He waved the lollypops around, showing them off to his men, who also broke into loud guffaws.

The Commander's mirth quickly faded, however. He made a slight gesture, and his men instantly stopped chuckling, too. The Commander's face returned to its grim countenance. He gave Michael a cold, hard stare and let the lollypops fall from his hand to the ground. He raised his right leg and stomped down hard on the lollypops with his big boot, crushing them. A split second later, a loud blast echoed through the jungle as the lollypops exploded, and the Commander was catapulted backwards. He crashed into several of his soldiers, knocking them down like bowling pins!

This was all the distraction Rocky and Piper needed. Before anyone could recover, they jumped to their feet and pounced on the rest of the startled soldiers, finishing them off with a series of precise mixed martial arts moves.

After the soldiers were dealt with, Rocky turned to Michael, smiling. "I kinda liked what you did with the candy again."

"Well, after the exploding chewing gum, I thought we could take the whole detonation theme to the next level."

"That's what I like about you, dude," Piper said, patting Michael on the back. You're like a boy scout—you're always prepared."

Rocky looked over at the Legerian commandoes' vehicles. "Wanna take some tires with you again?" he said, hoping the answer was "No".

Michael nodded affirmatively. "Yes, actually. That'd be great."

A short time later, Rocky, Piper and Michael sped through the jungle in the Commandoes' military vehicle with tires from the other cars strapped awkwardly to the hood. As usual, Rocky was driving as fast as humanly possible. He glanced at Michael, giving him a funny look.

"What?" Michael inquired.

"Didn't know you spoke North Legerian."

"I don't," Michael replied. "I just learned the needed words to do some reverse psychology on them."

Rocky couldn't believe what he was hearing. "So, you couldn't even order the Legerian national dish, soup with living fish and snakes, in their language?"

"Not even if I wanted to!" Michael said with a hearty laugh.

Rocky, Piper and Michael drove all day through the swampy North Legerian lowlands until they finally arrived at the capitol city. The huge metropolis, in spite of its enormous size and prominent role as the epicentre of North Legerian culture and politics, was an exceedingly drab place. Jimbo Jam's grandfather, the ruthless dictator, had demanded that all buildings be painted a dull grey and built in a boring, uniform style without any ornamentation whatso-ever. He did this to ensure that the North Legerian people would focus their hearts and minds on their obligations to the state, and not be distracted by useless things like interesting architecture or colors.

The streets were filled with people, but no one smiled or showed any emotion, least they get arrested by the police for displaying "selfish, self-indulgent, emotional excess." On the upside, there was practically no traffic, except for cheap bikes, on the nearly empty roads because almost no one in the impoverished nation, except high party officials, could afford to buy a car.

"My gosh, what a dreary, ugly place," Michael remarked as they motored past block after block of monotonous edifices and robotic looking people.

"I know, right?" Rocky said, shaking his head. "This dump makes Cleveland look good."

They continued onward until they finally arrived at the huge metal gates of the sprawling Presidential Palace. At the entrance, the trio showed their passports to the stoic guards, who, after many back and forth calls to authorities inside the Palace, finally allowed them to enter.

Rocky drove through the gates and continued into the main compound, escorted by several military vehicles…

… Watching Rocky drive into the Palace from his office window on the top floor of the Presidential Palace, General Takeshi, the ruthless, highly decorated head of national security, cursed quietly to himself—infuriated that Michael, Rocky and Piper had managed to get this far in spite of his best efforts to kill them. He picked up his phone and began launching on Plan B.

After they parked in front of the Palace, a dozen guards guided the three into a huge, round hall with many doors. The walls of the ornate room shined with elegant wallpaper decorated with real flakes of gold, and beautiful crystal chandeliers hung down from the high ceiling. The opulence of the Palace rivalled the magnificence of Versailles.

"Please, wait here," said a guard curtly.

"Sure," Piper replied, "we'll just chill and meditate on the word 'modesty' a bit." A second guard turned to them. "Sorry for your inconveniences on your trip. Apparently, word of your secret arrival had not been properly conveyed to all units of our air-defence forces. We apologize for any anxiety this may have caused you."

"Meh," Rocky said with a shrug, "it was nothing. Just some minor air disturbances. Besides, we like to get dirty for a living, don't we?!"

"Nothing like it!" Michael concurred merrily.

The guards stared at them stoned-faced, then abruptly turned and left the room—leaving the trio standing alone in the middle of the huge hall.

"Kinda neat place," Piper observed. "It's like, for sure, the largest waiting room I've ever been in."

"One can only imagine how big his other rooms must be," added Michael.

Suddenly, they heard someone giggling from behind one of the many doors. It sounded like a female voice. The giggling grew louder and louder, then suddenly, one of the doors flew open. Peggy, dressed in her sexy red dress with matching red pumps, came running into the room, almost tripping over her own feet. She rushed up to the gang, looking incredibly surprised and happy to see them.

"Oh, my God! Michael! Hey, so good to see you!" Peggy gave Michael and his cohorts a kiss on the cheek.

"These are my, uhm, my well-spirited, eager and most unique colleagues, Rocky and Piper," said Michael pointing at the two.

"Yeah, JJ told me, the three of you would drop by. You look a bit dirty!" she said, noticing how messy their clothes were from the plane crash and the subsequent fist fight with the commandoes.

"We exited the plane a little prematurely, met some locals and kinda took a detour through the jungle, first," Michael replied with an innocent shrug.

"Yeah, and then we kinda got lost," Piper said.

"The street signs are a mystery to me, here, too," Peggy explained. "It's that whole Legerian language thing. I never know whether to read it from left to right, right to left, or from the top downwards. Plus, I don't even speak the language. It's so... super foreign."

Rocky nodded in agreement. "That's exactly how I feel."

Just then, a male voice rang out, bellowing something that sounded like a cross between a grunt and a chant that went "HUAA!" and "HAAA!".

Seconds later, overweight Jimbo Jam, shirtless,

wearing nothing but blue shorts, came bounding in through another door. Peggy saw him and started giggling uncontrollably again.

"Oh, there he is! Gotta run. We've been playing hide and seek all morning."

"Good idea," Rocky noted with a smirk. "It's a great way to get to know each other better."

"Plus, it works up your appetite," Michael observed dryly.

Peggy laughed and took off running. Jimbo Jam immediately started ambling after her, but she quickly darted into another room, closing the door behind her again. Passing Rocky, Piper and Michael, Jimbo smiled and gave them a quick wave.

"Hello, Michael! Hello, Rocky! Hello, Piper!" Jimbo said in a friendly voice.

"Hey, skinny!" Piper shot back at him.

Jimbo let out a loud guffaw, amused by her insolence—which he found a refreshing change from the endless and tiresome fawning of his own staff. He gave them a big thumbs up.

"Make this place home. We'll talk soon!" he hollered back at them as he dashed through a door, "huaning" and "hassing" while he disappeared.

The trio stared at the door for a moment, not knowing quite what to say.

Finally, Rocky said out loud what they all were quietly thinking. "This is more bizarre than dreaming about a cat without hair."

Michael and Piper gave him smirks of agreement. "One surreal series of pinch-me moments!" Piper confirmed, "and I bet you, there's more to come!"

Suddenly, Peggy ran into the room again, being chased by Jimbo, who was still doing his "HUAA" routine. The pair dashed through another door and disappeared again.

Michael sighed. "Well… At least we now know for certain how dictators run their countries."

Just then, somewhere behind the closed doors, Peggy's giggling and Jimbo's "hua" sounds changed, they grew louder and more intense. It sounded like he had finally caught up with her, and *something* else was happening.

"Oh, my God…," Michael blurted out.

"Are they're going at it?" Rocky asked cringing.

Piper nodded. "They are definitely not playing Minecraft back there," she said as an icky look spread quickly across her face. The sounds of impassioned lovemaking grew louder and louder.

"What do we do?" Rocky asked, his face turning red. "Cover our ears?"

"It's not the most American thing to do," Piper agreed, "but let's!"

The three put their hands on their ears and waited awkwardly in the enormous room as the cries of lust and joy continued to ring out...

An uncomfortable hour or so later, Michael, Piper and Rocky found themselves sitting together with Jimbo Jam and Peggy in a beautifully decorated room eating lunch: sushi. Peggy was dressed far more appropriately—to everyone's great relief.

"So," said Peggy as she munched on a piece of Ahi tuna, "what do you think of the Palace? Pretty swank, wouldn't you say?"

Michael considered the question carefully. "It's mondaine," he finally said.

Peggy and Jimbo looked at each other, not quite understanding him.

"Wait... What?!" Jimbo suddenly shouted, "did you just call my gorgeous Palace, my primo crib, *mundane* like it's boring?!"

"No, I said it is *mondaine*," Michael corrected him.

Again, Peggy and Jimbo looked confused.

"It's French for *super elegant*," Michael explained.

"Oh, like you were using a difficult word to say how impressed you are—including all French people!" Jimbo roared.

"And those who accidentally speak French!" Michael said with a smile.

"Ooohhh…," Peggy and Jimbo said in unison, finally getting it.

Rocky added: "You know, Michael, the full professor-self, has this thing about all kinds of formulas, numbers and difficult words sometimes. Like these SAT words, which on a test are fun, when you can guess their meaning. But other than that, they are as mysterious as the origin of most of the UFO stories or the theory of the multiverse."

"Are we still talking about the awesomeness of my Palace?"

"Yep!" Piper confirmed.

"Definitely," Peggy completed the thought. "Your place, Jimbo, is cosmic. You just need to be able to see the connection."

"It's very deep. More than words can ever say!" Michael said affirmatively.

Jimbo proudly nodded along. "Thank you, guys. You're the best. And... oh, and by the way, since we're being deep and so very honest with each other. Sorry, that you had to wait that long. It is just, we got married yesterday, and we wanted to start making a family right away. I just wanted to get that apology off the table and off my plate. Speaking of which: How is the sushi, huh?!"

"Innovative taste," Rocky observed. "It makes you expect only good things."

Jimbo smiled, pleased at the compliment, then he turned to Michael. "Now, Michael, you and I are gonna have a competition climbing tomorrow. We want to create a huge, massive, fun and positive spectacle, with the both of us, you as Agent C2C and I as the bold leader, racing up two chimneys, to get every citizen on board for our transition to a full Cradle to Cradle economy and democracy."

Now, it was Michael who was smiling, "I'm impressed, Jimbo. Where did you get all these great ideas from?" Jimbo grinned at Peggy and winked at her.

Rocky was shocked. "You?!?" he said in surprise to Peggy.

"Yeah, I know, right?" Peggy replied, "cuz I'm just some dumb girl."

"I didn't mean it like that. I'm just surprised,

because… because….," Rocky trailed off, trying to come up with a plausible excuse.

"Because," Peggy interrupted, "you think I'm just the President's crazy, horny daughter, who's only aware of her erogenous zones?"

"And mine, too!" Jimbo interjected.

"That's kinda of obvious, sweetie, they do stick out. But as I was saying, I'm not just a sex-obsessed eco-warrior. I have a brain, too, you know. I've read over 10,000 books." She glanced over at Rocky, who was stuffing a wad of ginger into his mouth. "How many have you read, boomer?"

"Well, uhm, ma'am, by books, do you mean including comic books and what's written on cereal boxes?"

Jimbo let out a huge belly laugh and raised a closed hand asking Rocky to "dap" him. "You're just like me, bro!"

"I am not like you, but close enough."

They shared a laugh and banged their knuckles together. Peggy then pulled out a pair of strict looking glasses with a black frame and put them on her face. She sat up straight in her chair and spoke in a very serious, business-like tone.

"Okay. Now, guys, here is the deal: I will oversee

the transition of North Legeria to a Cradle to Cradle economy and democracy. I looked at all the data and statistics, number of people, the financial situation, infrastructure, GDP, and so forth. Thanks to my international network and my good relations with world leaders from around the globe, I have plenty of countries—including the U.S. and China—and many companies lined up to invest billions in North Legeria to make it a model state for Cradle to Cradle."

"We gonna blow this shit up like dynamite, yo!" cried Jimbo.

"Hell, yeah! I love it!" Michael said, pumping his fist.

Jimbo was literally beaming with delight now. He turned to Peggy with tears welling up in his eyes.

"I'm so freaking proud of you, bae! Before I met you, I was just another petty dictator, lost in his own ego-universe! But you changed me, baby…" Suddenly, Jimbo broke into a spontaneous freestyle rap:

> "You turned this no-good *player*
> into a climate-change-*slayer*
> and made him see the *light*,
> dissect every *layer*—

if we don't get it *right*,

we ain't got a *prayer*.

We need to stop serving up the *hate*

and bring love to the *plate*—

so, go with my *flow* and shout out *yo!*

Let's save this planet, before it's too *late*!"

"Man, that was raw, super unexpected and real," Rocky said. "This is extra hospitality. Some deep rhyme in the middle of lunch from the head-of-state host himself. You can make tons of friends with that. And we got to hear you live on top of everything else. You… you, my friend, are enormously flexible, gifted and a very special dictator, JJ!"

Everyone was deeply moved by Jimbo's impassioned, heartfelt words.

Jimbo snatched a glass of beer off the table and raised in the air for a toast. "Here's to you, baby, and to us—*the Dream Team*!"

Everyone raised their glasses, too, and drank a toast. Overcome with emotion, Jimbo suddenly grabbed Peggy and started kissing her. Soon, they were all over each other, swabbing spit and running their hands all over each other's bodies. As two lovers' passion grew more intense (and tremendously awkward), Piper coughed poignantly and spoke the words everyone was feeling.

"I think, I had enough sushi for today. Let's go meditate."

Michael nodded enthusiastically, tossing his napkin on the table. "Let's go quicker."

All three of them got up fast, leaving the room with the two lovebirds.

As he made for the door, Rocky muttered to the others: "I swear, they could repopulate the entire country if they had to."

Michael and Piper chuckled and headed out.

Unseen by the trio as they left the room, however, was a tiny security camera that had been hidden discretely behind a decorative potted fern near the door. The spy cam was feeding live video footage of the make-out sesh to the office of General Takeshi. The stern-faced security tsar was watching it in disgust along with a select group of very "Old-School" North Legerian military honchos. They looked like a parade of limping Halloween costumes, implementing the time-tested procedure of smoking cheap cigarettes to keep their lungs free from fresh air.

"Can you believe this shit?!!" General Takeshi hissed, pointing angrily at the video monitor (where Jimbo was seen yanking off his shirt and pants). "That fat little delusional brat wants to turn our beloved country into some kind of touchy-feely-eco-tourist trap!"

"Not only that," growled one of his mummified cronies, "he wants us all to give up our hard-earned power and status so he can turn North Legeria into a fucking *democracy*! In two months, we'll all be wearing rainbow-colored, tie-dye shirts and sandals, not paying attention to anything our citizens should not do and talking about legalizing dancing lessons! It's a betrayal of everything his by-the-book father and ill-tempered grandfathers built here and stood for!"

"What's wrong with him?!" wondered another old General, coughing like a horse. "This bastard even refuses to regularly smoke. He's not a team player! Has he gone insane to impress the younger generation?"

"He used to be such a nice little, mean boy. I remember when he blew up rats and frogs with these tiny pieces of dynamite. Just for the fun of it. He could have become a talented and feared leader!" muttered another strongman.

"I'll tell you what did this to him," growled the wizened commander of North Legerian air force, "it's that damn `hippity-hop´ music he listens to night and day. It's turned his brain into a creative, vibrating mush. This sorta thing puts new ideas and moments of awareness into one's mind. All that `yo-bro-yo-man´ random shit we now have to deal with!"

"No," said another wrinkled old fart. "It's the work of that devil-girl, the President's daughter. She's put an educated spell on him. I tried to warn all of you, she would be trouble, just like her hobby of wearing sexy micro-fashion. Now you see, don't you! She's clearly a spy, or a witch... probably both!"

"True...," agreed an ancient dude who was leering at the screen, staring at it intently like a dirty old man watching a free porn for the first time, as Peggy took off her top. "But you have to admit, you can understand the mysterious and mega-bewitching attraction—she is kinda eye-catching."

"That's why she is definitely a spy-witch!" another toothless grandpa general reasoned staring at the monitor like an overwhelmed, stressed-out bunny facing a very hungry snake. "She is engaging in the most severe form of war and witchcraft: Using love and intelligence to poison our leader with facts, fun and solutions to problems! This is pure evil!"

Several generals nodded grudgingly in agreement.

Suddenly, General Takeshi slammed his fist down loudly on a table. "Enough!!" General Takeshi screamed. "Our beloved nation is rhythmically being flushed down the shitter before our very eyes. We cannot blame it on the foreign media, our parents, mad animals in the run-down zoo or our genes. So, the time for debate is over—we need to act!!"

"And do what exactly, Takeshi? Go on an ironic hunger strike like some of our disoriented citizens occasionally do?" one of the old generals inquired.

"We need to launch *Operation Gangrene.*"

A hush fell upon the room. Several of the octogenarian military men audibly gasped.

"You can't be serious, Takeshi!" one protested, "that's too extreme. Things can go terribly wrong—like that expensive, but secret face-lifting operation our last leader's depressed wife had. Afterwards, she looked like one of these heavy Russian tanks—the really big ones we cannot afford—had rolled over her face. Twice!"

"Extreme danger calls for extreme measures!" Takeshi countered. "Even the loud Americans with their the-devil-might-care attitude left that room asap! That should tell you how intolerable this derailed situation of exercising one-on-one people skills is."

He gestured at the video monitor where Jimbo Jam was dancing around buck-naked to the delight of Peggy, unknowingly shaking his butt directly into the lens of the hidden camera. For Takeshi this was totally unpredictable, critical mass that was more high-risk than in an exploding power plant. He was feeling the meltdown in his mind already.

"If that's not subversive, I don't know what is. Soon, he'll have funny cartoon tattoos to jazz up his free-speech performances. We won't be able to fight that kinda leader with public relation stunts given our meagre budgets!"

The generals nodded solemnly in agreement.

"In war," General Takeshi continued, "when soldiers are wounded in battle, and a part of their body has become infected by *gangrene*—the doctors have no choice; they have to cut off the infected limp in order to save the patients. In this case, sadly, the head of our dear nation is hopelessly diseased. To save North Legerian and its people, that we've worked so hard for to keep innocent, we must act decisively and cut off our own head!"

"How does chopping off our own heads help?" one of the most senile, cloth-eared, five-star generals wondered. He was, by the way, having a hard time keeping his cheap denture (that, like bad breath, had been in the possession of his family forever) in place. His saliva kept dripping onto the floor. "Have you really thought this through, Takeshi?!" he muttered through the heavy fog of cigarette smoke. "What do you want us to do once our heads are severed?!"

"You idiot! I'm talking about getting rid of Jimbo Jam, the head of our nation, before these deadly, cool ideas he's infected with, *democracy* and *C2C environmentalism*, spread amongst the unprepared population and corrupt the entire country with information. Once Jimbo has been in-geniously eliminated, we will immediately assume control and rule North Legeria as a military junta, who will then also sacrifice itself voluntarily to eat his caviar and delete his Facebook account. Our first act will be to surprise arrest these absurdly trendsetting foreigners on the grounds of very bad behaviour, bad influence plus whatever else we find irritating. Next, we'll throw these forward-thinking American spies in prison and then have them all profession-ally tortured and then repeatedly shot—to treat them with respect and honour, even though they do not deserve this at all. We'll keep the President's daughter alive, though— she'll be useful as a bargaining chip to make the Americans lift all their economic sanctions against us. Because, it makes no sense to impose embargoes on a country like ours whose economy has been broken for decades. That's like asking people to jump up their own ass and die. We will force them to acknowledge that stupidity, and so we'll get our national pride back. That way, we will also restore reality-grounded reason to world politics and trigger years of open-ended negotiations and regain international respect. Our people will see that we are the very wonderful ones to represent them at countless, multilateral economic summits that are conveniently held in the vicinity of productive luxury spas on the global stage."

The gathered military men all nodded in agreement—imagining themselves resting selflessly in shiny, marble whirlpools to relax in between exhaustingly long meetings, where they would defend the few, overwhelmingly simple values of their country. Extreme poverty, one of the pillars of their society, like well-organized illiteracy and the lack of innovation, had kept their country stable and peaceful and vastly free from modern, confusing internet connections for generations! These hard-fought-for achievements—just like the heart-warming thought of young men and women marching for hours in especially stiff military formations—they were not ready to give up and erase from their radars, just because a young, crazy, fearless American gal was having great sex with their leader and had the nerve to talk to him afterwards about trendy eco ideas, too.

"Excellent plan, Takeshi," one general said. "Let's silence these annoyingly determined, energized people, who constantly regroup no matter what you throw at them, and who relentlessly talk about trees like they are actually *friends* with these organic wooden sticks frequently growing leaves in the countryside."

"Yes, yes! *Operation Gangrene* must be done, for the highest good of the nation."

"But how will this relief effort be accomplished?" asked one anxious general, while accidentally stepping on one of Takeshi's toes with his heavy wooden base.

"Ouch!" Takeshi exclaimed and angrily moved to the side.

"I know this all hurts. I can feel your aching pain, too, Takeshi," said the old fool. "But, let's face it, no matter how crazy he is, Jimbo still commands the undying loyalty of his personal, well-paid guards and palace staff. To them, he remains the boss of bosses. They're around him all the time, protecting him like a little, decorated puppy. Do you have a plan, General?"

A wicked smile spread slowly across General Takeshi's sharp, remorseless features—which usually meant he was trying to cover up one of his thorny gout attacks. But this time, he left no doubt that his mean, vampire grin was a direct, real-time, natural response to his superior mental brainstorming.

"Don't worry, comrades, leave everything up to me. I've already made the initial arrangements."

Takeshi turned back to the video monitor and sneered at Jimbo wiggling ass. "By tomorrow evening, North Legeria will be delivered from this fool's nonsense and put back on the path to traditional sanity…"

CHAPTER 9

PRESIDENTIAL PALACE, NORTH LEGERIA, NOON

At noon the following day, international news anchor, Ralf Richard Mann, welcomed his viewers to a "SPECIAL COVERAGE" segment from North Legeria. The headline in the background featured pictures of Jimbo, Peggy and Michael. A text above their faces read: ALL EYES ON NORTH LEGERIA.

"Welcome to all of our viewers from around the globe," Ralf began, "I'm Ralf Richard Mann with our special coverage from North Legeria. What a stunning turn of events! Not long ago, Jimbo Jam, the authoritarian leader of North Legeria threatened the world with his nuclear arms. Now, in a mind-boggling announcement from official North Legerian state media, he's revealed that he's married to Peggy Munger, the daughter of the U.S. President!"

At that exact moment, the same broadcast was being watched inside the Oval Office by President Munger—surrounded by his senior staff and his wife, the First Lady, Susan Munger. All were staring at the TV in total disbelief.

"How the hell did that happen? President Munger grumbled.

Totally energized, Ralf continued the live coverage from North Legeria:

"Together, the young couple wants to establish a Cradle to Cradle economy in their country. To start things off with a bang, today they are hosting the first North Legerian 'Positive Event' to celebrate Jimbo's abdication of absolute power and to start the immediate transition to democracy and Cradle to Cradle." Ralf paused for a moment and looked directly into the camera. "I think, I speak for many viewers out there when I sum up my reaction to this incredible breaking news by saying simply: Wow!"

On the screen, there was a "whoosh" transition sound effect as the report cut away from Ralf to reporter Sandy Splash broadcasting live from a large public square in the middle of the North Legerian capitol. Behind Sandy, the space was filled with cheering people. Two huge chimneys could be seen, standing prominently in the middle of the square, stretching into the sky like two gigantic straws.

"The pictures you're seeing are live from North Legeria," Ralf told the audience, "as we join our very own Sandy Splash, who is, as you can see, standing by in the midst of the cheering crowd in The People's Square. Sandy, what can you tell us? Fill us in. What is the atmosphere like down there?!"

On the screen, Sandy held her finger to her ear-piece and shouted into her microphone so she could be heard above the din of the roaring crowd.

"Good morning, Ralf!" Sandy yelled. "What a beautiful day. Couldn't be better, and the crowd here is so fired up. I just spoke to a woman and her children, and they all said, they cannot remember a day, when they were so happy."

The cameraperson panned over to a woman with her

two children who waved merrily and cheered into the camera.

"Truly an extraordinary event today!" Ralf interjected. "Now, what is the purpose of those two chimneys in the background, Sandy?"

"Ralf, that is the big event we are all waiting for: The race to the top of these two chimneys between leader Jimbo Jam and Cradle to Cradle co-founder, currently the *Sexiest Man Alive,* Agent C2C, Michael Braungart."

"Did I hear you correctly, Sandy, did you say, *race?*" asked Ralf incredulously.

"Yes, Ralf, apparently the two men are going to have a contest, climbing to the very top of these enormous chimneys to symbolise the triumph of humanity over heavily subsidized, polluting fossil fuels."

"Fascinating," Ralf replied, "does the winner get anything special?"

"Apparently, the two men have made a personal wager. Michael Braungart has asked President Jam to make a special donation to his C2C water reclamation project in Brazil if Agent C2C wins."

"What if the hip-hop-expert President scrambles to the top first, rapping `Yo-yo'?"

"Then, Ralf, Michael must relinquish his hard-earned, undisputed title of *Sexist Man Alive* and bestow it upon President Jam."

"Wow, those really are high stakes, Sandy. This should be quite an interesting contest to say the least…"

Meanwhile, back at the Presidential Palace, everyone was busy getting ready for the big climb. Inside a special dressing room, Jimbo and Peggy were warming up by making out, of course. Jimbo was wearing a pair of sweatpants, high-top tennis shoes and a swanky, extra blingy, shiny golden Fubu jacket that his wardrobe assistant had ordered to be flown in directly from Hong Kong. Peggy was ecstatic over his outfit—and him.

"I love you, chubby face," she cooed softly between kisses. "I'm so proud of you. You're doing the right thing."

"I've never felt so right before," Jimbo replied. "For the last five days, we've only been doing the right thing."

"I know you have, sweetie, but right now, I'm just talking about you climbing onto the top of the chimney and winning. I mean, I know we have a higher goal here, so I don't want to get too caught up in the whole competition thing, but I really want you to smoke Braungart's butt!"

"Don't worry, bae," Jimbo said with a confident grin, "it's in the bag. I'm in the best physical shape of my life. Mop-top will be eating my dust the whole way up. After I've won the climbing competition, we'll get a special bracelet made from the finest jewelers in Paris—oh-là-là-bien-sur—and on it we'll inscribe: *Jimeggy*."

Peggy smiled and gave him a sensual kiss on the lips.

"That's the spirit."

In another dressing room, in the guest area of the huge palace, Rocky and Piper stood in front of Michael, who sat slumped in a chair, looking pretty anxious. They were in the middle of trying to give him a pep-talk. Rocky was bent down, staring deeply into Michael's eyes—it almost looked like he was trying to hypnotize him.

"No pain... No fear of heights... No mercy!" Rocky said slowly.

Michael nodded and took a sip from a water bottle.

Piper then bent down and spoke softly into his right ear. "I want you to clear your mind of everything. Think of nothing, except a picture of that chimney, and how you're gonna be the first to reach the top. You feel nothing but power. You're the force that can do anything."

Michael laughed. "Are you trying to turn me into a force-sensitive Jedi or something?"

"Correct you are," Rocky replied, doing a Yoda

voice. "Climb the tall chimney and win you must!" Rocky then took out earpieces and handed them out to everyone.

"Here. Put these in your ears. That way we can communicate. I'm still not convinced that the hardliners will just stand by and watch their regime fall."

They all put in the earpieces. Piper opened a small steel case that she had brought into the dressing room. Inside were her collection of artificial AI ladybugs. She showed them off to Michael and Rocky.

"Also, I already planted a lot of these babies outside. They're programmed to spot danger and neutralize it—just in case."

Michael plucked one of the robotic ladybugs out of the case and looked it over, amused. "Adorable. You took them with you?"

"I never travel without them," Piper replied.

"And I still got one of these bad boys…," Michael said as he pulled out one of his explosive lollypops from his pocket.

Piper took a step back. "Be careful with that."

"Don't worry," Michael said, waving the lollypop around casually in the air, "I'm an award-winning chemistry professor."

Rocky patted him hard on the back. "Exactly, you're

priceless."

Suddenly, without warning, the door to the dressing room burst open, and three menacing-looking soldiers waving machine guns stormed into the room! The armed men were followed by two old generals (who were cronies of General Takeshi) and a creepy-looking Medical Doctor, carrying a sinister-looking black bag. Michael's face went pale. Rocky, however, looked more annoyed than scared by the sudden turn of events.

"I really don't like it when people burst in and start changing the subject!" he said casually to the intruders.

The soldiers ignored him. They pointed their guns at Michael, Rocky and Piper, screaming at them in North Legerian to raise their hands in the air.

Piper slowly raised her hands up, but first, she managed to subtly press a button on the side of her steel case. This switch activated her ladybugs. As the soldiers continued to bark orders at them, three of the little winged robots fluttered out of the briefcase and darted inside the soldier's gun barrels—without them even noticing. Rocky, Piper and Michael, of course, did take notice and gave each other subtle looks.

Rocky started talking back to the men aiming deadly weapons at them. "I hope you speak some English," he said, angrily. "Cause I'm telling you to lay down your weapons slowly, like you mean it!"

"Stay calm, guys!" Piper chimed in. "Don't trip over your subconscious or anything. We're kinda nervous guests and not pleased with the level of your room service at this moment in time. It's a bit too *testosteronic*."

The soldiers, old generals and the creepy-looking doctor all looked at each other for a moment, then burst out laughing.

Rocky nodded, unfazed by their mocking guffaws. "Glad you like our choreography instructions."

"And…," added Michael, "spoiler alert: Your guns are no longer operational."

Again, the soldiers laughed. One old general started bellowing at them in bad English. "On your kneecaps, you merit-less worms!"

"We don't have time for this crap, papo!" Piper said to Rocky.

Michael concurred. "Let's get creative, guys."

"I say," Rocky replied, "we do some extra head-butting!"

With that, Rocky suddenly grabbed a soldier by the ears and smashed his big, Texas sized forehead full-force into the man's nose. A loud WHACK rang out as skull met bone! The soldier staggered backwards, in a daze, with blood spurting out of his broken hooter. He dropped his weapon and collapsed to the floor.

Piper instantly jumped into action, throwing a series of lightning-quick punches, punctuated by a perfectly targeted groin kick that found it's mark in the crotch of another trooper. He went down in a heap as well.

The third soldier tried to rake them all with machine gun fire, but his weapon jammed and made a horrible grinding noise when he pulled the trigger. Smoke, not bullets, came wafting out of the end of the barrel. Rocky spun around and clobbered the dude with a big upper cut to the jaw that sent the unfortunate man flying into the wall—out for the count!

Seeing their goons totally neutralized, the two old geezer generals and the creepy doctor all backed up against the wall, cowering in fear.

"Please… Don't hurt me!" one of the generals whimpered pathetically.

Rocky sneered at them. "Okay, now, you employees of the month, who look like reanimated evil jokes from the bowels of hell. Who ordered this shitshow? Don't be a tough crowd. Just tell me!"

The generals and the doctor looked at one another;

they were freaking out, but no one dared to speak.

"We'll never talk!" snapped one of the old coots, defiantly.

"That so, pops?" Rocky replied, sounding very unimpressed.

He balled up his hand into a big fist and grabbed the wrinkle-faced prune who had spoken up by the front of his shirt. Instantly, he waved his clenched hand menacingly before the man's darting, terrified eyes.

"Thing is, this angry fist never fails to impress. Tell me, or I'll transport you someplace even more dark and painful. It will be your worst wish fulfillment. So, who is behind this, grandpa?!"

The General's knees went limp as a nightmarish image of Rocky turning his testicles into a set of ping-pong balls flashed through his mind. He hung his head in shame.

"Takeshi…," he muttered reluctantly.

Just then, JJ's guards, alerted by the commotion, burst into the room pointing guns in every direction.

"Welcome boys, perfect timing!" Michael said with a smile. "We just had a coup plot against President Jam occur in here that needs your immediate attention."

The guards surrounded the rogue soldiers and shoved the barrels of their rifles underneath the old generals' chins. This worked as a great motivational tool for Rocky as he continued his interrogation.

"Go on, I'm listening!" Rocky demanded.

The old general finally decided that further hemming and hawing really wasn't in his best interest. "General Takeshi ordered that you were to be drugged and put under hypnoses to make you kill Jimbo Jam," he sputtered out.

"Wow," said Piper, rolling her eyes. "Apparently, they've given it some real thought."

JJ's head guard turned to Michael. "We're so sorry. We will immediately arrest Takeshi and his group and tighten security."

"That sounds like the best of both worlds!" Michael replied.

"Sweet!" Rocky chortled as the guards marched the defeated plotters away. "This was the perfect warm-up routine to get the blood flowing. Now, I'm like totally ready for the big event. Let's take the party outside."

A carnival-like atmosphere had descended upon The People's Square that morning. Jimbo Jam's rap songs and other motivational music was blasting from loudspeakers set up on towers. The enormous crowd was screaming and yelling at the top of their lungs, waving flags with both Jimbo and

Michael's faces printed on them (although, it must be said, they were mostly rooting for JJ as he was their President and the "home team").

As JJ's rhythms echoed through the air, Michael, accompanied by Rocky and Piper, Jimbo Jam and Peggy, (wearing a tight dress)—emerged from the palace and began walking the short distance to the two chimneys. The sight of the contestants made the assembled throng go totally bananas. They shrieked and jumped up and down as if they were at the finals of the World Cup. People in the front rows crushed up against the barricades, forcing the police to strain every muscle to hold them back.

JJ sauntered up to the edge of the crowd and started slapping high-fives with his delirious fans. Then, he whipped out a microphone from his shiny gold Fubu jacket and started spitting out a freestyle rap:

"JJ's here,
So, lemme hear ya'll cheer!
Throw your hands in the air
Show the world that you care!
Let's rock! Make it pop!
Shake your booty like it's hot!
Cuz, it's a race to the top

And we just can't stop!

Lemme hear you say, 'Yo!'"

Jimbo cupped his hand around his ear and listened as the crowd shouted back in unison: "Yo!"

Jimbo and the crowd did a few more back and forth calls and responses before he jumped back into his rap.

"Whoa!

There you go!

Didja hear that sweet flow?

The people want some mo'

They're ready for the show

Says who? Says me!

JJ—the king of MCs

And my shaggy-haired homie

Agent C2C!

So, let's get the party on track

And take this planet back!

Relax, eat some snacks

DJ, pump the volume to the max

Watch us soar like regal-eagles

And climb like crazed-cats

As we go on the attack

And dust these chimney-stacks!"

To the crowd's utter delight, Jimbo then "dropped the mic" and began busting crazy cool hip-hop dance moves across the plaza. After awing the throng with his gyrations, (punctuated by a big crotch-grab), Jimbo spun around and pointed at Michael, obliging him to join him. Michael turned red and shook his head, mouthing "No, no—not me!" But the excited crowd wouldn't have it. They screamed encouragement at Michael, not just imploring, but demanding he join the dance.

Finally, reluctantly, Michael stepped into the middle of the square next to Jimbo and started doing some awkward dance moves. Michael's dance routine was, at first, a bit insecure, but the crowd didn't care at all. They laughed and cheered wildly—they were loving every minute of the show. This got Michael to suddenly loosened up. He started really going for it, hopping around to the beat and even shaking his booty in an attempt to "twerk"—which got the spectators boiling even more. JJ joined in, and the two began busting out freestyle moves together, rocking the audience in unison.

As all this was going on, Rocky and Piper were busy

scanning the crowd for possible additional coup plotters. Not seeing any threats, Rocky turned and stared at the chimneys, making sure there was nothing out of the ordinary with them. They looked normal at first glance, except, Rocky did notice two hatches on the side of the chimneys, located about two thirds of the way up. Rocky turned to one of the guards accompanying them and pointed at the flaps.

"What are those hatches for?"

"We built them to install a surprise mechanism inside the chimneys to celebrate the winner of the contest with a beautiful, popping gesture," the guard said proudly.

"That's cool," Rocky replied, "a happy bonus at the end. That'll be great for everybody."

Piper, meanwhile, checked her special "spy watch" which signaled to her that all ladybugs were activated. The micro drones were discreetly hovering all over the People's Square, scanning the area. She checked the live video feed from each one and then gave Rocky a thumbs up—everything looked okay. Rocky nodded back to her and then signaled Peggy, who then gestured to Jimbo that it was "showtime".

Jimbo and Michael finished their impromptu dance and took a bow as the crowd gave them a thunderous round of applause. They each took a moment to catch their breath and stretch a little before heading over to the base of the two tall chimneys.

Michael and Jimbo shook hands and took up positions at a white starting line next to the ladders leading up the chimneys.

Peggy walked out a few yards in front of them, holding a green flag. She raised it over her head—like she was starting a drag race. The crowd went silent. Jimbo and Michael crotched into running stanches and tensed up in anticipation of making a big start.

Peggy shouted out: "Ready...? Set... GO!!!" Then she brought the green flag down with a whoosh!

The crowd screamed! Michael and Jimbo sprang into action, leaping out of their starting positions as fast as a chubby rapper and a chemist could, running hard to reach the two ladders. Dramatic music (composed by Jimbo himself) began thumping out of the speakers to heighten the excitement. Jimbo reached his ladder first, but Michael was only a step or two behind him. Almost in unison they began scrambling upwards, making the long ascent along the sides of the lofty chimneys.

At the base of the colossal smokestacks, Rocky and Piper screamed encouragement to the *Sexiest Man Alive*.

"Come on, Michael!"

"Whoo-hoo! Jimbo! Go, dawg, go!" Peggy cried.

In the apartment halfway across the world, Michael's personal assistant, Chantal, was watching the amazing spectacle with a group of friends. Chantal was gnawing on her thumbnail, on the edge of her seat, literally shaking with excitement.

"Oh, my god. Oh, my god. Oh, my god!" Chantal gasped. "This looks so real!"

In the Oval Office, President Munger watched the neck and neck race with his wife and key staff members. He was staring at the TV in disbelief, looking like a serious A-student, who had just misspelled the word "flappergasted". Munger just couldn't wrap his Presidential "I-m-the-most-powerful-guy-in-the-world" mind around the fact that Peggy and Jimbo were the global tabloid's number one favorite people and had been named the world's "Most Inspiring" couple by leading magazines. *"What kind of a world was this,"* Munger thought to himself, *"where young, clever, creative people could steal the freaking show from seasoned heads of state and their army of talkative advisors, unstoppable spin doctors and overpaid consultants?!"*

"How did that all happen?" he muttered incredulously.

A nervous staff member tried to offer up an opinion. "Well, sir, I think perhaps your daughter and Jimbo Jam only had an extremely short dating window and were... well... basically humping away the possibility for any kind of rejection phase between them and got married right away. Way too little time for any international diplomacy to prevent this."

President Munger stared at the staff member like he'd like to rip his tongue out several times. The staff member, sensing the event horizon of the emotional black hole coming his way, gulped, broke his gaze and stared at the ground. "Sorry, sir."

Munger turned to his CIA director, Robert Jordan.

"And what's next?"

"The *audio-surveillance* I got from the CIA, MI6, and Interpol half an hour ago indicates very strongly that you'll be a granddaddy next year."

President Munger groaned loudly and buried his face inside the palms of his hands. The First Lady, smiling reassuringly, put her hand on her husband's knee to calm him down.

"Don't worry, dear. We'll get them the best

babysitters…"

Meanwhile, back on the side of the chimneys, the race was incredibly close; Michael and Jimbo were neck and neck! The two were about halfway up by now. Michael had been doing fairly well up to this point, but it was here that he made a major tactical error—he looked down. Seeing just how high he was, a height so lofty that (to him) the huge crowd looked like ants swarming around an anthill, made Michael's nervous system go into total shutdown mode. He instantly froze up and stopped climbing.

Seeing his dismay, Rocky shouted into his earpiece mic, trying to encourage Michael. "Keep going, numb-nuts! The only way down is up!"

But Michael stayed locked in place.

Jimbo glanced over at Michael clinging desperately to the ladder, paralyzed with fear. He laughed and shouted to him: "Loser!" Jimbo continued ambling up his ladder, taking a decisive lead. However, Jimbo's snarky taunt had the effect of snapping Michael out of his delirium—he could never let an insult go by unanswered.

"Thanks for the good vibes, sunshine!" he yelled back at Jimbo.

Michael suddenly spun into action. He started

climbing again, going faster than before. In fact, he quickly caught up to Jimbo and took the lead!

At the base of the tower, Peggy watched Michael getting ahead of Jimbo through a pair of binoculars and shouted into her own megaphone.

"Yo! Jimbo! Get your booty in gear, babe! Don't let flop-top beat you!"

Jimbo looked back down and saw Peggy standing at the base of the chimney tower. To inspire him, Peggy had pulled her dress off to reveal that she was wearing a red-hot bikini underneath.

"Dang, bae!" Jimbo shouted down to her. The thought of Peggy greeting him in that sexy swimwear in the winner's circle inspired Jimbo to dig deep and find another gear. He started climbing like a crazed Spiderman on Red Bull and soon caught right back up to Michael.

Rocky threw up his hands and turned on Peggy, pissed off by her bikini stunt. "Hey, that's doping!" he yelled at her in dismay.

Peggy just shrugged back at him, innocently. "I'm 100% natural."

Watching the back and forth contest in her apartment, Chantal was so excited that she was literally jumping up and down.

"Oh, my god. Oh, my god. Oh, my god!" she chanted. "This is like the good luck message of my last fortune cookie coming true!"

In the International News Channel studios, the race played live in the background as Ralf called it for viewers like a color sports commentator.

"Now it's Jimbo in the lead... wait, no, the *Sexiest Man Alive* is making his power move, now it's Michael ahead... but hold on, here comes Jam picking up speed, he's ahead by a nose again—boy, this is a close race!"

At that moment, high up on the chimney towers, Jimbo was extending his small lead over Michael. Perhaps it was the thought of Peggy in her hot bikini, or the fact that, in spite of his girth, he was feeling several light-years younger since Peggy (wearing tight, red bikinis) had come into his life, but he was definitely starting to pull away. He could literally feel the energy of Peggy, her mind-boggling, fortunate bikini (so little can do so much) and his people all rooting for him to succeed. He was already seeing himself as the glorious, hip-hopping winner, who had—at least physically—outsmarted the genius professor with the fuzzy hair. The only problem that JJ could imagine was whether or not it was humanly possible to also thank a red, hot, totally compostable bikini for the emotional support and carrying him to victory.

However, just as he had clambered up his ladder, faster than ever with his lucky-charm energy, and passed by the hatch, it suddenly sprang open! Out of the trapdoor below JJ, someone tossed out a small object. The oblong shaped item whizzed by Michael and landed in the middle of the People's Square far below. It made a small explosion and began spewing out a cloud of thick fumes—it was a smoke grenade! Nearby spectators began screaming and panicking as the smoke filled the air and stung their eyes.

Rocky whipped his head and looked at Piper. "Is that a weird part of the ceremony?"

Piper shook her head, looking very concerned. "I don't think so…"

The smoke cloud was so thick that in a couple of moments it was impossible to see a thing. Piper lifted up her high-tech spy watch and quickly tapped in some instructions. In seconds, several of her ladybugs came flying in and started spraying anti-smoke chemicals. This helped clear some of the haze, but Michael and Jimbo were still obscured by the artificial fog hovering in the air.

Rocky shouted into his earpiece mic: "What's happening, Mike?! We have no visual of you!"

"I think someone dropped something out of the hatch below JJ. But everything looks fine up here," Michael reported back.

Peggy sensed danger, however, and screamed into her megaphone. "JIMBO! SOMETHING'S WRONG! LOOK OUT!!"

Way up on the chimney, Jimbo heard Peggy's warning cry. He stopped climbing and paused to look around. Just then, a man suddenly popped out of the open hatch, holding a gun: it was General Takeshi!

"SHIT!" Michael cried. He called up to Jimbo: "Look out, man!"

Jimbo looked down, and saw General Takeshi pointing his weapon at him with a triumphant, sinister smile on his lips.

"Takeshi? You back-stabbing bastard!" Jimbo sneered at him.

"You're the traitor, you arrogant little punk!" Takeshi barked back at him. "You've betrayed everything your beloved grandfathers and father stood for! All, so you could chase some tail!"

"Guys!" Michael tried to whisper inconspicuously

to Rocky and Piper. "We have a situation unfolding up here. It's an old train-wreck-type uniform dude with an angry gun. Could be worse than a family dispute."

However, down below in the loud chaos, Rocky and Piper could not hear much, other than the last words that sounded like "family is good".

"Did Michael just say `family is good´ up there?" Piper shouted towards Rocky.

"Yeah, sounded like it," Rocky replied wondering. "Kinda awkward moment to say that, though, unless he's making a professor-joke about all the crazy chaos."

Up on the chimneys, the drama kept moving along to the next chapter. JJ rambled on as if Takeshi was a reasonable sounding-board for some reality-based information:

"It's not about Peggy, bro—all she did was open my eyes a bit and help me listen to what's inside my heart." Jimbo paused for a moment, and he gave Takeshi a sincere, sympathetic look. "Look, I feel you, Takeshi. I loved dad and grandpops, too, but they were like from a different era, yo! The world's changed a lot since they were the big OG's around here. We understand so much more about science and nature and the impact humans have on the environment. We can't go on doing the same stupid shit we did in the past, bro—otherwise we'll kill ourselves off as a species and everything else on this beautiful planet. We need to start learning how to work with Nature's Cycle instead of against it, or there won't be a North Legeria anymore. Can't you see that, homes?"

"I'll tell you what I see," Takeshi hissed, "a spoiled brat who's too stupid to see he's been brainwashed by American propaganda. *Climate Change* is just a hoax dreamed up by our sworn enemies in the West to fool us into slowing our industrial production even more, so we'll be weak and vulnerable—then they can invade us! And you fell for it completely, you incompetent fool! You've brought ruin and shame upon us all!"

Jimbo stared at Takeshi, thunderstruck by his mind-numbing paranoia and idiocy. He shook his head and said with a sigh: "You've gone totally cray-cray, bitch."

Takeshi's jaw went tight. His eyes lit up with silent rage. "That's the last insult you'll ever make." Takeshi lifted up his gun and took careful aim at Jimbo's head. "Time for you to die, fat boy!" He squeezed the trigger…

…but at that precise moment, one of Piper's ladybugs flew right into the barrel of Takeshi's gun. Takeshi pulled the trigger, but the mechanism mis-fired and the weapon exploded! Takeshi let out a yelp of pain as the pistol shattered in his hand and flew out of his grip with lots of dark smoke shooting out of his barrel like a jet, blackening his face.

Watching the action on the live video feed, inside the International News Channel studios, Ralf didn't quite understand what he was seeing unfold.

"Oh, my God!" he shouted excitedly. "This looks like an ambush on Jimbo Jam!" Then, Ralf let out a chuckle. "LOL! Don't get too nervous, folks, no doubt this is all part of Jimbo's well-choreographed show. Looks pretty real. Well done!"

Back in the Oval Office, however, the President looked stressed—like he had to instantly succeed in dividing 3,517,6 by 24,8 without a calculator. He turned to the CIA Director. "This can't be good, right?!"

Robert Jordan shrugged his shoulders. "It's a bit weirder than my cousin's gothic, punk-style wedding with the illegal appetizers."

In her apartment, Chantal was both nervous and annoyed by all of this.

"I don't want to be judgmental or coming across as boring," she said to one of her friends, "but this is a little much! What a waste of free air-time."

Back up on the side of the chimneys, Jimbo looked at Takeshi, nursing his hurt hand and stuck his tongue out at him.

"That's what you get, loser!" taunted Jimbo, pointing at the smoke pattern on Takeshi's face. "Talk about being embarrassing globally. Now you look like you have a butt crack all over your forehead."

But Takeshi wasn't finished. He growled at Jimbo and whipped out a knife!

"Oh, shit…," muttered JJ.

Takeshi put the knife between his teeth and tried to climb out of the hatch onto Jimbo's ladder. Jimbo gulped and tried to move upwards as quickly as he could, but his foot got caught in one of the rungs of the ladder. Jimbo tried to yank it loose, but he was in full-on freak-out mode and in his panic couldn't figure out how to untangle it.

On the ground, Piper and Rocky saw what was happening. Piper tapped her wristwatch and sent three flying ladybugs at Takeshi. The Ladybugs were pesky, but the little drones were more of an annoyance than an obstacle to

Takeshi, and he continued to climb out of the hatch as he swatted them away.

"This is not inspiring!" shouted Rocky in distress.

A little way down the chimney, Michael looked up and saw what was happening; Takeshi was about to amble out of the hatch and climb onto Jimbo's ladder and stab him. Thinking quickly, Michael took out his last lollypop.

"This is getting too personal and cutting edge. I'll deploy my last lollypop!" he cried into his mic.

"He's really doing the Braungart-lollypop!" Rocky repeated.

Piper went pale and shouted into her wristwatch: "No, Michael, don't—That's too dangerous!"

But Michael had an idea. "Not with the hatch open!" he replied.

With that, Michael tossed his chemically enhanced and fine-tuned candy high up into the air. It flew past Takeshi and went right inside the open hatch where it struck the inside of the chimney and exploded! The blast went off inside the chimney, so Jimbo wasn't hurt at all. The chimney shook, which helped him to untangle his foot, while he was able to also cling to the rung of his ladder and hold on.

Takeshi wasn't so fortunate. The resulting explosion was channeled right out of the open hatch. The concussive blast hit him square in the chest and catapulted him off the chimney! Takeshi plummeted through the air, screaming like a little schoolgirl before landing hard in the branches of a nearby tree. The crowd, most of whom did not realize that this *was not* part of the show, started applauding.

On the International News Channel broadcast, Ralf couldn't help making an inspired quip out of the situation:

"Looks like Jimbo's assassin just turned into a real tree-hugger! Wow, Agent C2C saved the day once more. How sexy can a man get! This spectacle is the perfect everything!"

Back in her apartment, Chantal was jumping up and down in front of her TV and doing karate kicks.

"You show'em, Michael!" she yelled at the screen.

In the Oval Office, President Munger and everyone with him breathed a collective sigh of relief. President Munger turned to Robert Jordan, the CIA Director, and quietly said:

"I want to know that lollypop recipe and have every Secret Service agent carry one. That's an executive order."

His wife patted him on the back. "I'm so proud of you right now," she said. "Suddenly, our whole family is starting to make so much sense."

At the bottom of the chimneys, the crowd was going crazy. Rocky and Piper were hugging and pumping their fists in triumph. Rocky looked up proudly at his brother and gave him two big thumbs up. Quickly, he tapped his microphone.

"Nice, very nice, bro!" he said sounding both relieved and genuinely impressed. "I guess you do need a challenge once in a while to go full genius."

Piper nodded in agreement. "Great move to cut the bullshit factor."

"Thanks, well, you know me—I'm all about cutting the crap," Michael replied.

"How's my boy, Jimbo, doing?" Rocky inquired.

"Let me check," said Michael.

He looked up, Jimbo was near the very top of his chimney, but he was looking pretty shook up from his encounter with Takeshi. His face had turned a greenish shade, and he wasn't climbing anymore, just clinging to the ladder with both hands.

"Jimbo?" Michael called out. "How you doing there, bro?"

Jimbo let out a loud burb (that tasted like his breakfast) and shook his head dismally. "Not so good...," he groaned. "I can't go on, bro. I feel a bit queasy, like I'm gonna hurl!"

"Come on, buddy!" Michael responded in a reassuring voice. "You can hurl later. Let's finish the race and do some serious geopolitics first!"

But Jimbo didn't move. He was shaking. Yet, suddenly, they both heard a familiar voice call out through the loudspeakers in the People's Square. It was Peggy! She had stopped the music and gotten on Jimbo's microphone.

"JIMBO! Don't give up, boo! I love you! Just do the right thing!"

The crowd let out a collective "Ahh," touched by her declaration of love. Some began to chant: "JIMBO! JIMBO!" Soon others in the throng took up the mantra, which quickly spread until everyone in the plaza was crying out: "JIMBO! JIMBO!"

With the crowd and the woman, he loved, urging him onward, Jimbo took a deep breath and began to climb again. Michael smiled and started scaling his ladder as well. Side by side, on either chimney, they ascended in unison, determined to reach the top. Nothing, apparently, could stop them now! Or so it seemed...

Suddenly, they both heard a loud cracking sound ring out.

Jimbo stopped and looked up; just above his head, he saw fractures forming around the metal bolts that held his ladder to the side of the chimney.

"Oh, crap…," Jimbo muttered.

"Not good!" Michael hollered out.

Then, all at once, the bolts holding Jimbo's ladder tore loose from the side of the chimney! His ladder broke away from the smokestack and started falling backwards.

"JIMBO!!! NO!!!" Peggy cried into the microphone.

The entire crowd let out a gasp and screamed in terror as they watched Jimbo's ladder bend backwards at a forty-degree angle. Jimbo was dangling from it now, suspended in mid-air, many stories above the ground as he desperately clung onto what was left of his ladder with both hands!

Rocky turned and yelled at some nearby guards: "He's gonna fall! Scramble a helicopter! Get a rescue team up there! Find a net! Don't just stand there! MOVE!" The guards quickly ran off to get some help.

"There's no time for all that!" Piper said, pointing up at Jimbo. "That ladder can't hold him, it's gonna break!"

Right on cue, the ladder that Jimbo was desperately holding on to suddenly let out a terrible groan, and one side of it snapped in two! The part of the ladder that didn't snap continued to bend sideways, however. It swung around towards Michael and stopped short from the side of Michael's chimney. Jimbo hung there, just below Michael's feet, panting heavily, praying that the ladder wouldn't break any further. Michael looked down at Jimbo.

"Bad English isn't your only problem anymore, huh?!" Michael quipped, trying to calm Jimbo down.

"Don't make me laugh!" Jimbo replied unsteadily.

In the People's Square, far below, guards and staff were trying to inflate a huge safety cushion.

Rocky got on Michael's earpiece. "We're inflating a crash pad, bro! But we'll need a few seconds. Can Jimbo hang in there for a little longer?"

Michael looked over at the part of the twisted ladder that was still attached to the chimney. It was bending and cracking before his eyes.

"Negative, Rocky!" Michael replied nervously. "Hold on, I'm gonna try something." Michael looped his arm around the rungs of his ladder to secure himself, then started taking off his belt.

Rocky, Piper and Peggy saw what Michael was doing through their binoculars. The move surprised them.

"Stripping like Peggy isn't gonna help," wondered

Rocky aloud.

"How do you know?!" Peggy shot back at him.

Back up on the side of the chimney, Michael carefully removed his pants and a shoe with indestructible, super strong C2C laces and tied them all together with his belt, making what looked like a makeshift "lasso". He then began to swing it around in circles.

Jimbo looked up and could see what he was trying to do. "Are you effin' crazy?" he said incredulously.

Michael nodded affirmatively. "Yes, and... you're welcome!"

With that, Michael threw the lasso at Jimbo. The lasso flew towards Jimbo, caught a piece of the broken ladder and dangled just in front of him. Michael wrapped the shoe at the end around his ladder, helping to hold it in place.

"Grab it, Jimbo!" Michael ordered.

Jimbo let go of the rung with one hand and grabbed the lasso, wrapping the improvised rope around his arm. Michael got a firm grip on his end of the temporary safety line.

"Now, the fun part, my friend... let go and swing onto my ladder. I'll hold you."

Jimbo looked at Michael—you sure?

"Don't worry, I got you. I promise!" Michael

insisted.

Down in the plaza, the crowd was completely silent, except for a few people who were weeping—everyone was holding their collective breath. Jimbo's fingers were starting to lose their grip on the one rung he was still holding. He was running out of time...

"C'mon, Jimbo!" Michael pleaded, "trust me, we're gonna save the world together. I'm the *Sexiest Man Alive*, all because of a joke. So, you can get into the survival mode worthy of a hip-hop dictator turned married eco warrior!"

These last words seemed to stick with Jimbo. He gritted his teeth, let out a yelp and let go of the broken ladder. The makeshift lasso went taunt as his full weight fell upon it. Michael strained with all his might, to keep himself from being pulled off his ladder as Jimbo swung over to the chimney.

Jimbo was suspended briefly in mid-air as he swayed away from the collapsing ladder. Then, he bounced gently against the side of the chimney just below Michael. He quickly reached over and grabbed Michael's ladder with both hands, securing himself safely.

"I got him!" Michael cried into his earpiece mic.

"Agent C2C did it! Jimbo's safe!" Rocky screamed to the crowd.

An enormous roar went up from the assembled multitude. People hugged and kissed each other as Michael and Jimbo climbed the last few remaining ladder rungs, headed for the top of the chimney. Tears streamed down Peggy's face as she cheered on her husband's triumph. On the International News broadcast, Ralf let out a loud sigh of relief.

"Thank goodness!" he said breathlessly. "After a near coup attempt that almost took the life of President Jam, thanks to Michael Braungart, aka Agent C2C, it looks like these two unlikeliest of heroes are going to reach the summit safely. All I can say folks is three meaningful letters: WOW!!"

In her apartment, Chantal had stopped jumping around and had collapsed on her sofa, murmuring raspy "yays"—her voice (and nerves) completely shot after all the heart-pounding drama.

In the Oval Office, everyone was cheering and slapping high-fives. Even the bummed-out President Munger managed to smile.

"Good work, Michael!" he said, "you saved my son-in-law—oh, God, did I really just say that? It sounds like raw magic no one has ordered, or meeting a deadline if you don't have to. What if this JJ comes to the White House and starts rapping right next to me? The world's gonna call us `The President-Dudes', like forever, yo."

His chief of staff, Wilmer Clint, turned to him. "Sir, this might ease your concerns regarding your brand and history's judgement of your presidency a little. I just checked in with Sally Martin your head pollster. She says your approval ratings are already trending way up thanks to this."

"Really?" said the shocked President in surprise. "That's the kinda math I like."

Clint nodded. "It's crazy, I know, but people love TV, the Earth and the prospect of nutrient-rich world peace, and thanks to your daughter, they're giving you credit for all that. It's like winning two beauty pageants without competing in them. Can you imagine if Jimbo and Peggy re-celebrate their wedding on the South Lawn? Your numbers will go through the freaking roof like your lucky number is infinity—and all of that just in time for your re-election campaign!"

"I guess, that's the unexpected upside," replied the President relieved, "of being the emotionally stable and stead-fast President-Dad of a highly innovative, rebellious daughter. I feel like there are even countless young people out there who start thinking I'm officially and seriously cool."

The First Lady gestured to the TV, where the broadcast was showing Peggy cheering at the top of her lungs and wiping away tears of joy from her face. She looked ecstatic.

"Can you believe it, Sydney?! Our daughter has revolutionized geopolitics, speed dating, election campaigning and cheerleading at the same time," the First Lady said with a proud smile.

Back up on the side of the chimney, Michael and Jimbo were at the end of their climb. Michael paused for a moment near the top and looked down at Jimbo, checking to make sure he was alright.

"Are you O.K., chubby face?" he asked.

Jimbo gave him a thumbs up. "Thanks, man. I owe you one!" Jimbo nodded upwards, gesturing to the top of the chimney. "Go for it, homie. Do it for the team!" he said.

Michael smiled back at Jimbo and started climbing again.

When Michael reached the very top, he stood up with his hands over his head and saluted the crowd below.

Rocky, Piper and Peggy, along with the audience in the plaza and people watching his victory all around the world, let out a deafening cheer. Then, all of a sudden, the sound of gears and a mechanism engaging rang out. Michael felt a slight vibration beneath his feet as a blossoming cherry tree on a rising platform emerged from the middle of the chimney—the surprise bonus for the winner!

Michael jumped onto the branches of the cherry tree and was lifted up with it as it rose into the air and crowned the ugly smokestack with a halo of pretty pink flower petals. It was an ideal ending to the intense race and a symbolic, seminal moment that the world would remember for a long, long time...

CHAPTER 10

GENERAL ASSEMBLY, THE UNITED NATIONS, 10 AM

President Munger stood at the podium before an excited crowd of the world's diplomats, who were eagerly awaiting his much-anticipated address to the UN General Assembly. Sitting in the audience among the United States delegation was his proud daughter Peggy, his wife and, of course, Michael, Rocky and Piper. Jimbo Jam was sitting with the North Legeria delegation a short distance away. He glanced over at Peggy and blew her a kiss. She winked back at him as her father cleared his throat and began his speech.

"Good morning, ladies and gentlemen," President Munger said. "It is, as always, a great honor and privilege to stand before you today in this incredible body of representatives from nations across the world. This past week has seen some of the most tumultuous, and yet, promising events in recent history. All of us, myself included, have come through these dramatic trials with a deeper appreciation and understanding of the environmental crisis facing the world. As dire as our situation may appear to be, we do have solutions within our grasp to solve this human-made disaster of climate change, one of the many idiotic consequences from polluting our environment. The one resource that is truly sustainable on this planet is human intelligence, ingenuity and our unflinching determination to solve difficult problems."

A round of enthusiastic applause went up around the chamber. President Munger waited politely for the clapping to die down, then continued:

"Thank you. The United States has always been a world leader in times of crisis. Like the action packed, `sleep-faster-work-harder´ California Governor Arnold Schwarzenegger said at this very podium in 2007, speaking about California's pioneering new environmental and climate laws: `*California is moving the United States beyond debate and doubt to action.'* Our great nation, at its best, is indeed a `*shining beacon of light on the hill'* as my esteemed predecessor, former President Barak Obama, once famously said in 2015 in Malaysia. In the spirit of this noble sentiment, the United States is committed to leading the charge against global warming and, therefore, ending pollution. To this end, I am pleased to announce that the U.S. will fully support the transition to a Cradle to Cradle, positive circular economy. Let's create a prosperous future for all together!"

Thundering applause rose from the audience.

"You rock, man!" Jimbo shouted out.

"Finally, you're cool, dad!" cried Peggy. She punctuated her approval by sticking her two index fingers in her mouth and letting out a booming whistle.

Michael, Rocky, Piper and the others, including the First Lady, "whoohooed" loudly! President Munger laughed and grinned at his daughter and Jimbo. For the first time, he was feeling genuinely happy for them.

"Right back at you guys!" he called out to Peggy and Jimbo from the podium. "You're the best! We're family, weird and kicking ass!"

The assembled diplomats burst out laughing and

continued clapping enthusiastically. Jimbo and his delegation rose to their feet and gave President Munger a standing applause. They were soon followed by the rest auf the cheering assembly.

LOS ANGELES, SET OF THE JENNY JAY TALK SHOW, 5 PM

Jenny Jay, the thirty-two-year-old, good-looking host of the popular late-night show, sat patiently behind her interview desk, reviewing info cards as she waited for a cue from her on-set producer, Aaron, that the next guest was about to join her. She heard a beep in an earpiece she was wearing and glanced at Aaron, who signaled her by holding up two fingers. Jenny nodded, put down her index cards and looked up, smiling, at her in-studio audience.

"Ladies and gentlemen," Jenny said in an energetic, welcoming tone of voice, "our next guest has been named the *Sexiest Man Alive*. Others also extremely seriously call him 'James Bond's and Jason Bourne's real-world brother.' He just recently won the world's weirdest competition climbing in North Legeria, and today, here he is! Please welcome: Agent C2C, the co-founder of the Cradle to

Cradle design concept, Michael Braungart!"

The studio audience clapped and cheered as Jenny's band played a happy jingle, and Michael Braungart came running out onto the stage, wearing a pair of over-sized, funny-looking colored sunglasses that would have made Elton John proud, waving enthusiastically to the crowd. To the audience's delight, instead of heading for Jenny's couch, Michael sauntered over to the band, picked up a spare guitar and started playing along with the musicians.

The band members found his antics utterly hysterical and started belting out a Rock `n´ Roll song. Michael went with the flow, jamming away on his borrowed guitar like a poor man's Jimi Hendrix. He punctuated his inspired performance by dramatically sliding to his knees after hitting the final note and holding up the guitar over his head. The audience went completely gaga over it. Michael took an elaborate bow, handed the guitar back to the band and finally joined Jenny.

"Great to see you, Michael!" Jenny said as Michael took a seat on her white sofa.

"Great to be here!" Michael replied.

"So, Michael…"

"Yes, Jenny?"

"Obviously, wherever you go, the *Sexiest-Man-*

Alive tag is with you. What's it like being the sexiest dude on earth wearing those effective anti-villain colored glasses?"

"It just gets better every day!" Michael said with a grin.

Both of them laughed along with the audience. Then, Michael did something that shocked everyone; he took off his crazy glasses and ate them!

"Oh, my God, you just chowed down on your glasses!" Jenny cried out in astonishment.

"That's what being fully recyclable is about!"

"Wow. You want some Sriracha sauce with that?!!" Jenny said with a smirk.

"You want a bite?" Michael asked.

Jenny at first made a comical face, but the audience egged her on shouting: "Do it!"

Finally, Jenny shrugged. "Sure, why not? I mean, not to brag or anything, but I have eaten my share of clothing before—mostly edible undies, though."

Michael handed her a piece of his glasses. Jenny popped it in her mouth and chewed slowly, then smiled. "Ummm… interesting… I have to admit, it's not half bad, tastes kinda like sugar-sweet chicken."

"Want some more?"

"No, I'm good, thank you, your eyewear is delicious, but I'm trying to cut down on between meal snacks. I'm on a diet, apparently. But really nice demonstration, Michael. Well then, moving on from eating our clothes to current events, let's talk about more good stuff: at the United Nations last night, something amazing happened. Tell us about it."

A more serious, thoughtful look spread across Michael's face. "A life-defining moment happened. 195 countries signed a binding agreement that says that all member states will now implement Cradle to Cradle principles."

On a video monitor behind Michael and Jenny, footage of the signing ceremony played. A photo then appeared, showing President Munger with his happy wife, Peggy, Jimbo Jam, Michael, Rocky and Piper standing proudly together at the signing table, holding up the signed document.

Jenny's in-studio audience let out a roaring round of applause. Jenny waited for the hoopla to finally die down, then continued: "Wow, what a happy global family. That's truly great."

At this very moment, a loud explosion echoed through the studio, smoke shot up from all sides, the lights flickered. Jenny screamed, like the rest of the audience. Michael looked shocked, too.

From the ceiling, thick ropes dropped down to the floor, with two soldier-type personal descending on them an instant later. The two operatives wore black face masks, and once on the ground, they started to secure the premise with their machine-guns—sending everyone into shock again. Then, a black SUV came speeding onto the stage. Secret Service men jumped out from the front and opened the doors to the backseat.

"What the…!" Jenny stammered, while her producer laughed knowingly.

Out of the car stepped America's happily smiling first family, accompanied by their streetwear-savvy son-in-law, JJ. The two masked soldiers revealed themselves as, of course, Piper and Rocky, grinning like the First Family and waving at the crowd. Out of their guns came colorful candy flying to the audience.

"HOLY SHIT! HOLY SHIT!" Jenny cried. "Did you know that?" she asked Michael.

"No way!" he shouted back, totally overwhelmed, while Rocky ran over to him, lifting him up in the air. "Love you, man!"

"Can you ever do anything not insane!" Michael laughed.

The audience went crazy, standing up, cheering and

applauding.

"I'm sooo gonna kill you, Aaron!" Jenny yelled laughingly at her producer, still shaking a bit from the surprise. "Wow!" she gasped once more. "I'm speechless, and my ass is sweating. How often does this happen!" Then she turned to the First Family. "Welcome, first-ever-more-awesome family!"

"Hey, gorgeous!" President Munger greeted Jenny Jay. "Remember how I said at the UN that we'll be a family to kick ass and change the planet!"

"Yes, sir, and congratulations on the diplomatic language that I can finally understand!"

"Do you mind if we tear down your stage here after the show?" Munger inquired.

"Hell, no! And please beat my prank-expert producer over the head with it, too. Other than that, I just hope you know where you're going with this!"

"You bet! We're gonna tear it down and replace everything with new, fully recyclable, super healthy materials!"

The audience cheered and whistled even more.

"Wow! Wow!" Jenny gasped. "This is sooo sexy!"

"It really is!" Michael said smiling.

JJ jumped in and rapped out loud:

"Listen! YO! The man has more to say:
Something great about tomorrow to be
announced here today!"

"Go ahead, Mr. President, sir!" Jenny said.

"Starting tomorrow, my daughter, Peggy, will, at the age of 18, become the first, youngest-ever Secretary of Commerce and Environment. The future of the young generation is happening NOW!"

The band started playing a loud rock jingle. President Munger went over to his daughter, gave her a kiss, then he kissed his wife and high-fived JJ and the others. Finally, he shook hands with Michael. Meanwhile, the SUV was removed from the stage and more seats where placed next to the white guest sofa.

"All right. Tonight, I'm definitely not gonna use the word `normal´ anymore. Man, these are powerful feelings here. Have a seat, you weird, adorable bunch of nutjob guests!" Jenny laughed.

They all took a seat smiling and giggling.

"Yeah," Michael said joyfully. "I think these moments are gonna get like a gazillion hits on Instagram."

Jenny feigned a look of jealously. "I know, this is

totally gonna bury my unfiltered `I-look-wasted´ selfie with George Clooney at the Oscars—damn you people! Have you been inhaling freaking vitamin crazy lately! Have we ever had such a fantastic moment on TV, folks!"

"NOOO!!!" the audience shouted and applauded.

"First time ever I feel great when a crowd yells `NOOO´ at me," the President commented with a big smile.

"Seriously, though, this time in history is truly amazing!" Piper reckoned and Rocky continued: "It's like an Einstein Moment, 'cause Einstein said that we humans have to change our thinking to build a constructive future."

"Yes, it's happening!" Michael said, sounding hopeful. "When my awesome brother here starts quoting Einstein, you know the world will be different!"

"IT'S HAPPENING!" JJ repeated. Then he started making out heavily with Peggy.

"Oh, wow! I thought these were just super exaggerating tabloid rumors going around about these two lovebirds!" Jenny snorted with laughter.

"No!" confirmed the First Lady. "We cannot even go out to dinner with them. Restaurants are starting to seat us in private rooms."

"This is so romantic!" President Munger said.

"We're in love!" JJ confirmed sitting up straight

again.

"Love is universal!" Peggy added.

"And live on TV! I'm so happy for you, guys. We could all use a little more reassuring body language once in a while!" Jenny quipped. "Awesome. I mean, that love theme of yours is way less bananas and definitely way healthier than all the billions of tons of waste we humans have produced. That toxic stuff cannot even kiss my ass. I gotta say, my kids totally love the whole Cradle to Cradle idea, and they keep asking me stuff like: `Mom, why did we ever produce toxic waste in the first place?!' And you know what? They're right! Producing toxic waste is such a strange idea, especially as no other species on this planet does that."

Michael nodded in agreement. "It's crazy, right? Producing waste or even less waste is making the wrong idea perfectly wrong... Boy, it's like wanting to be the raunchy king of booger town."

The audience laughed again.

"But that's the past," Jenny said, looking at her audience. "We are, ladies and gentlemen, together with this wonderfully inspiring, unnormal First Family heading into a smart future of a world with a booger-free, Cradle to Cradle, circular economy—"

Michael finished her sentence. "—where all eco-intelligent materials in climate-smart production cycles will be fully recyclable, serving as positive nutrients in either the bio- or the technosphere, benefiting both people and planet."

The audience again rose to their feet and applauded. The band started playing an upbeat tune again. Michael got up, so did Jenny Jay and the others.

"Ladies and Gentlemen: Michael Braungart!"

Michael and Jenny shook hands and then started doing a little dance together—with all the others joining in. Softly, Jenny whispered in Michael's ear:

"My clothes are really compostable!"

"So are mine!"

324

Title Song to the Novel

Music & Lyrics by George Hohbach
Arrangement by Alfred Huff

VERSE 1
Agent C2C
He takes no cover
He's the perfect lover
`Cause he knows
Why Nature grows
`Cause he goes full cycles only
Full cycles only the way all thrives
In our lives
Full cycles only

BRIDGE
C2C
Rock `n´ Roll
The world's your Oyster
The world is whole
We live
Cycles positive
Oh, Yeah!

CHORUS
Two spheres it is
C2C won't miss
Oh, yes
Because it is something
That can see us through
Turn around what we do
Because it is something
More good for you.

More good for you.
More good your you.

VERSE 2
Agent C2C
He does not scare
His mission is to dare
`Cause he knows
Why Nature grows
`Cause he goes full cycles only
Full cycles only, all goes round
Wholeness is found
Full cycles only

BRIDGE
C2C
Rock `n´ Roll
Our best agent
Accomplishes all
We live
Cycles positive
Oh, Yeah!

CHOURS
C2C won't miss
A goal or a kiss
Oh, yes
Because he's someone
Who can see us through
Turn around what we do
Because he is someone
More good for you.
More good for you.
More good your you.

C2C won't miss
A goal or a kiss
Oh, yes
Because he's someone
Who can see us through
Turn around what we do
Because he is someone
So close to you.
So close to you.
So close to you.

THE C2C MUSIC VIDEO

Title Song to the Action Comedy Novel

music & lyrics: George Hohbach
arrangement: Alfred Huff

Intro

Cmaj7   Dm7   Em7   G7   Cmaj7   Dm7

Verse

A-gent C 2 C   He

4 Em7   Dm7   G7(sus4)   Fmaj7   Dm7   G7

takes no co-ver He's the per-fect lo-ver   'Cause he knows Why Na-ture grows

6 Dm7 Em7 G7 G13   Cmaj7   Dm7   Em7   Am7

'Cause he goes full cy-cles on-ly   Full cy-cles on-ly   the way all thrives   In

Bridge

9 Gm7   C7   Fmaj7(add9)   Am7   Em7

our lives   Full cy-cles on-ly.   C 2 C   Rock-'n'Roll   The

12 D7   Fmaj7   Dm7(add9) Dm7 G7   C   G7   C C7

world's your Oy-ster The world is whole   We live cy-cles po-si-tive   Oh yeah!

Chorus

15 Cmaj7   Dm7   Em7   Fmaj7   Gm7   C7

Two spheres it is C 2 C won't miss Oh Yes!   Be-cause it is some-thing   That

18 Dm7   G7   Gm7   C7

can see us through   Turn a-round what we do.   Be-

20 Fmaj7   Dm7   C Dm7 G7   G13   C

cause it is some-thing. More good for you.   More good for you.   More good for you.

328

PART 2

About
Michael Braungart
& Cradle to Cradle
with illustrations and photos by George Hohbach

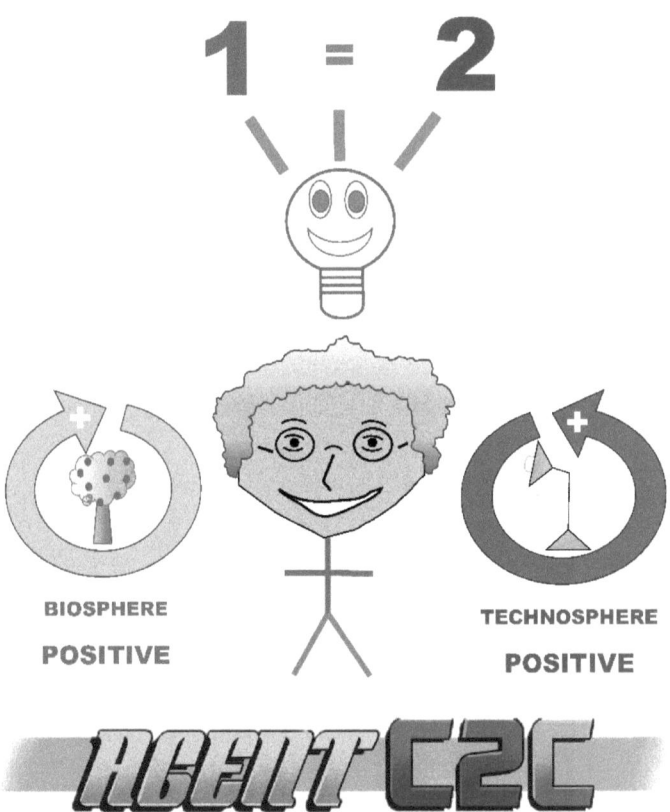

Why the Cradle to Cradle design concept makes companies, people and governments partners in striving for eco-intelligent, climate-smart solutions

MICHAEL   BRAUNGART,

who is the source of inspiration

with his life and ideas for this

book, is a world-renowned

chemistry professor who has

taught at several U.S. institu-

tions, including Carnegie Mellon University in Pittsburgh,

Pennsylvania and the Darden Business School in Char-

lottesville, Virginia. He is the founder and CEO of *Braun-

gart EPEA,* the international Environmental Protection En-

couragement Agency, co-author of two international best-

sellers and co-founder of the groundbreaking, *eco-intelli-

gent and climate-smart* CRADLE TO CRADLE design

concept. He developed this thought-leading idea with his

U.S. partner and co-author, the pioneering environmental

architect William McDonough. Internationally, Cradle to

Cradle is usually known by the abbreviation C2C. The phi-

losophy and school of thought of Cradle to Cradle stands

for the following: high-quality materials of a product are fully reused again when a product reaches the end of its usability cycle (end-of-use). This is in stark contrast to the linear thinking of "Cradle to Grave" (take-make-waste) which signifies that products, which have reached the end of their usefulness are either immediately thrown away to become waste, which generally pollutes the environment, including the emissions of greenhouse gases, and causes valuable raw materials to get lost, or, through the downcycling of the ingredients of the product, the materials increasingly lose their quality and then (just a little later) must also be disposed of as waste. Michael Braungart, along with his American partner William McDonough—with whom he founded the C2C-consulting firm MBDC in Charlottesville, Virginia and the Cradle to Cradle Products Innovation Institute in San Francisco, California—has received numerous international awards for his groundbreaking work benefitting human society on a global scale including the U.S. Environmental Protection Agency's "Presidential Green Chemistry Challenge Award" in 2003. In 2007, *Time* magazine named both Michael Braungart and William McDonough "Heroes of the Environment". With the revolutionary Cradle to Cradle design concept, companies around the globe are more and more succeeding in continuously reusing innovative, increasingly safe materials of the highest quality in biological and technical cycles. Using energy-effective and efficient eco-intelligent and climate-smart production processes—based on, e.g., utilizing ever more renewable, local energy, saving energy via reusing precious materials or keeping carbon contained in the recycled substance—ensures, at a progressive rate, that all used, valuable substances and production processes in both the biosphere and the technosphere are **permanently safe from the outset**. Thus, the process creates more and more positive effects for people and the environment, and ensures that resources are handled responsibly.

Therefore, short-term thinking and long-term oriented actions are supposed to get united constructively and innovatively, just as the smallest levels (the molecules, the individual human being) and the larger levels (nature, the planet) are brought into greater harmony. The goal of Cradle to Cradle is to present the positive-holistic unity pattern of nature in the form of a simple, highly effective (eco-effective) and also efficient approach to mankind. This allows each individual human being to create a growing **POSITIVE FOOTPRINT** on the planet, since the Cradle to Cradle design concept, from the start, makes all materials and production processes safer and more conducive for planet and people, and aims for continuous improvement—including solutions for climate change.

This is one of the central, socially relevant topics of the present and future of humanity, and the Cradle to Cradle community continues to grow steadily across the planet. With Cradle to Cradle, the concept of the modern "circular economy" has been defined cyclically and positively with nutrient cycles in a consistent fashion, and linked to the idea of continuous, comprehensive global improvement and up-cycling. Today, numerous international organizations, such as the United Nations, the G20, the European Union and leading international companies, institutes and foundations use the term "circular economy" in all areas. The term "circular economy" was also used in the 1990s in the Chinese translation of the book *Cradle to Cradle* as part of the subtitle, so that, in China, Cradle to Cradle is often equated with the term circular economy.

Cradle to Cradle has already been featured in various museum exhibitions and internationally acclaimed documentaries. The support for Cradle to Cradle is growing: from the E.U.—e.g., the Belgian E.U. presidency—to China to the U.S.

In the context of the groundbreaking *California Green Chemistry Initiative*, California Governor Arnold

Schwarzenegger, in 2010, supported the launch of the C2C Products Innovation Institute (a U.S. non-profit organization managing the C2C certified Products program). One of the top recommendations of the California Environmental Protection Agency in 2008 was: "To Move Toward a Cradle-to-Cradle Economy." Today, California is the world's 5th-largest economy. Former U.S. President Bill Clinton wrote the foreword to Michael Braungart's and Bill McDonough's second book *The Upcycle.* The E.U. has funded several Cradle to Cradle projects like the international *Cradle to Cradle Network Project* (2010 - end of 2011), the international *Cradle to Cradle Islands Project* with partners from countries surrounding the North Sea (2009 - end of 2012) or, e.g., *BAMB* (Buildings as Material Banks, beginning 2015), a project that integrates C2C concepts in the building sector. China took inspiration from Cradle to Cradle for, e.g., its *Circular Economy Law* in 2008. The World Economic Forum substantively embraced

Cradle to Cradle methodologies in 2014 for its *Project Mainstream* to scale up the circular economy.

More and more governments and government agencies, as well Hollywood greats, musicians and fashion designers, entrepreneurs and cities like San Francisco or Venlo in the Netherlands are employing C2C principles. Venlo, for example, uses C2C techniques in its city hall to help to purify the air. A wide assortment of foundations, organizations, universities, and people around the world, support the groundbreaking Cradle to Cradle design concept. It allows people to be good and positive to themselves as well as to nature, to celebrate creativity, abundance and thus infinite possibilities along with diversity and beauty. In short, Cradle to Cradle enables people to be happy about their own existence!

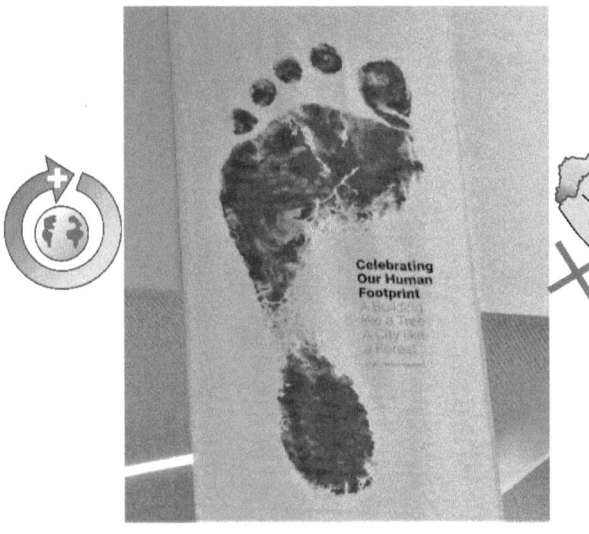

THE POSITIVE FOOTPRINT

**The huge poster of the C2C exhibition at the Biennale Architettura 2016 in Venice,
presented in the lobby of the Libeskind-Building during the C2C Congress 2017.**

Celebrating Our Human Footprint

A Building
like a Tree
A City like
a Forest

Michael Braungart's Idea:

with the help of the C2C design concept based on the cyclic scheme of Nature, humanity can create a positive, growing ecological footprint, that everyone can be happy about.

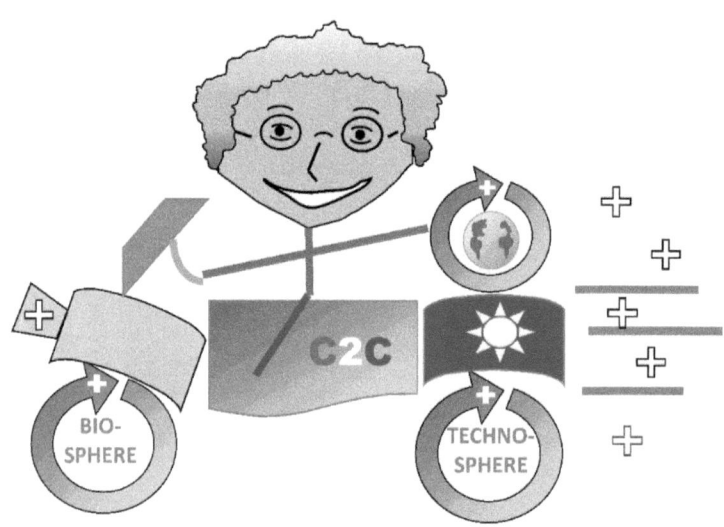

Inspirations from Michael Braungart's life for the story

• For the Cradle to Cradle design concept, Michael Braungart was inspired by the example of nature as well as from various branches of science and the humanities and from different eras and cultural environments from all over the world. Various aspects of human existence, such as joy, fantasy, beauty or meaningfulness, also belong to Cradle to Cradle.

• Michael Braungart once climbed a chimney.

• Michael Braungart once fell in love with his chemistry teacher during his school years, and to woo her...

• ...he taught the whole class chemistry!

• His parents had a colorful, joyfully growing garden, for which they first had to pay a fine and then later got an award for it.

• Michael Braungart loves to use humor in his lectures.

• He loves using ants as an example for humankind because they're so intelligent and cooperate together so well and live constructively with nature.

• He thinks the cherry tree is a wonderful example from nature for positive abundance, from which the environment benefits.

• C2C is not about being "less bad to the environment and to oneself", but rather about designing and optimizing things to be positive for humans and the planet from the start, so that the human, ecological footprint can always keep growing for the benefit of people and the environment.

"There is no zero waste. It's all nutrient."

Michael Braungart at the C2C Congress 2017

"We can look to Nature (…) as our teacher. Nature gave us the correct recipe."
Michael Braungart & William McDonough
(The Upcycle, North Point Press, 2013, p.221)

The source of inspiration for this novel

Michael Braungart

is the internationally renowned, award-winning co-founder of the groundbreaking Cradle to Cradle design concept. He is a chemistry professor, multiple bestselling author, sought-after speaker and the founder and CEO of *Braungart EPEA*, the international research and consulting institute for Cradle to Cradle solutions and their implementation. Throughout the world, companies in all fields, are—thanks to C2C—increasingly succeeding in designing and manufacturing products in an environmentally-intelligent way that benefits both humans and the environment. For many years now, C2C has received continuous support from numerous Hollywood greats and celebrities around the world. More and more governments, government agencies, regions, cities and organizations rely on C2C to achieve improvements for humans and planet. For this book and the story, Michael Braungart was the source of inspiration with his life, his thoughts and his work.

The authors

George Hohbach

studied law and has collaborated for many years with a talent and literary agency in Beverly Hills. His art—music, paintings, books, documentaries—is presented domestically and abroad in galleries, educational centers, companies and museums. On the connection between Albert Einstein's groundbreaking, symmetrical equivalence principle, the ensuing mathematical principles and Cradle to Cradle, he has written numerous system-theoretical analyses, a summary of which was published by a science publisher. He is the head writer of this book, illustrated both the title sequence as well as the 2nd part of the book and wrote both the music and lyrics for the novel's song *Agent C2C*.

Ehrengard Hohbach

is a former physician with a specialty in holistic medicine. She gave numerous lectures, seminars and courses on that topic. Her expressionist, symbolic paintings—also inspired by C2C and Einstein's findings about symmetry—are exhibited in galleries, companies and museums domestically and abroad. Her artistic and literary work was covered several times on radio programs as well as in newspaper articles.

Scott Marcano

is the critically acclaimed and award-winning writer/director/producer and CEO of Diablo Productions. His film and television credits include movies for MGM and The Walt Disney Company, including the cult environmental comedy *Bio-Dome*. For this book, he was also the project manager.

The illustrator
Juan Romera

is a well-known illustrator from Argentina who is working with publishers around the world. He has also collaborated on several critically-acclaimed graphic novels with Diablo Comics.

The Co-Translator
Robin Palmer

is a veteran Hollywood agent, producer and television network executive who has worked in the business for over 30 years. Robin Palmer is also a produced screenwriter and has published numerous Young Adult novels with Penguin Random House and Simon & Schuster. She currently resides in Louisiana where she teaches in the film department of Tulane University.

The Musician
Alfred Huff

is a well-known German musician, film music composer and the CEO of Medienhaus Mainz. He produced the sheet music for the novel's song *Agent C2C* as well as both its arrangement and recording.

ACKNOWLEDGMENTS:

Such a book does not come into existence without the enthusiastic participation of many people. But we wish to single out a few here: First of all, many thanks to Prof. Braungart for allowing us to write the book based on his life and groundbreaking ideas. Many thanks to Gülcan Yurt, office manager at *Braungart EPEA*, for the always friendly and warm support, as well as to Patrick Meiß, personal advisor to Prof. Braungart. Many thanks also to both our inspiring project manager Scott Marcano, our imaginative illustrator Juan Romera and our most supportive musician Alfred Huff for their productive collaboration and to author Robin Palmer for her excellent help with the English translation. Finally, our thanks to our agent Lloyd Robinson for the comprehensive support of the project.

Appendix

Cradle to Cradle
& Albert Einstein's Findings About Symmetry

Cradle to Cradle (C2C):
The design concept by chemist Michael Braungart and architect William McDonough is based on the recognition that nature understands itself as a unity. This unity or wholeness of nature shows itself, e.g., in holistic unity-cycles, like nature's diverse and countless nutrient cycles. C2C uses two different such unity-cycles, a nutrient cycle for the biosphere of nature and one for the technosphere, the realm of man-made technology. Since both seemingly different C2C cycles are structured the same way and have the same goal—namely, to design and produce things in an environmentally intelligent way so that they are positive for humans and the planet right from the start—the C2C holistic unity-cycles, and thus also the products, form a scientifically based, simple, harmonic and, therefore, symmetrical whole. Since chemistry plays a connective role between physics, biology and other fields of science, it has the potential—as in C2C—to translate basic natural laws into positive-holistic concepts for humankind.

Albert Einstein:
The physicist Albert Einstein was born in Ulm (Germany) in 1879 and died in 1955 in Princeton, USA. From a very early age he was interested in mathematics and spent long hours studying the field with a family friend. At age 12, he became convinced that nature could be understood as a simple mathematical structure. With the help of symmetry (sameness, equality, equivalence, unity, balance, invariance, i.e. remaining unchanged, harmony) as a simple, beautiful, mathematical idea—scientifically discovered in nature—Einstein later achieved his groundbreaking successes of the theories of relativity. These theories created a unified, harmonious understanding of the universe in which the laws of nature are the same for all observers. One of Einstein's great achievements was that he took simplicity seriously

and revealed this elegance in nature. At first, Einstein wanted to give his theory of relativity the title *Invariance Theory* because *invariance* represents "remaining unchanged", i.e., "staying the same" and thus stands for symmetry.

The well-known mathematician **Emmy Noether** (1882-1952) underpinned the fact that the laws of nature are always invariant and thus also confirmed Einstein's findings and the significance of symmetry in nature. Einstein called Emmy Noether the most important woman in the history of mathematics.

The discoveries of Einstein, which provide the foundation for a scientifically based, modern holistic view of the world, are built on the findings of **Galileo Galilei** (1564-1642)—who also began to scientifically reveal the importance of sameness or symmetry in Nature—and **Isaac Newton** (1643-1727).

For Einstein, fantasy and imagination were even more important than knowledge, and he described the mysterious in nature as the most beautiful experience and as both a fundamental feeling and as the source of science and art alike. The various disciplines which—according to Einstein—should enrich the life of every human individual, he saw as the branches of a single tree.

In addition, symmetry considerations also point to the oneness of Nature (the cosmos) on the level of quantum mechanics.

Further Reading

C2C:
- *Cradle to Cradle* by Michael Braungart & William McDonough, Vintage, 2009
- *The Upcycle* by Michael Braungart & William McDonough, North Point Press, 2013
- *Creating Buildings with Positive Impact* by Douglas Mulhall, Michael Braungart & Katja Hansen, Technical University of Munich, 2013

C2C inspired Circular Economy, Environment, Climate:
- *Completing the Picture – How The Circular Economy Tackles Climate Change*, a report by the Ellen MacArthur Foundation, 2019
- *The Green Industrial Revolution* by Woodrow W. Clark II & Grant Cooke, Butterworth-Heinemann, 2015

Circular Economy & the UN's 17 Sustainable Development Goals:
- *The Circular Economy – A User's Guide* by Walter Stahel, Routledge, 2019
- *The Circular Economy – A Powerful Force for Climate Mitigation*, a report by Material Economics and its partners
- *Closing the Loop – The benefits of the circular economy for developing countries and emerging economies* by Alexandre Gobbo Fernandes, a project by EPEA Brasil, Tearfund, NuRes, Tearfund, 2016
- *The Trillion Dollar Shift – Achieving the Sustainability Goals* by Marga Hoek, Routledge, 2018

Albert Einstein:
- *Ideas and Opinions* by Albert Einstein, Three Rivers Press
- *Einstein – His Life and Universe* by Walter Isaacson, Simon & Schuster, 2008

Galileo, Newton and other great Scientists:

- *From Galileo to Gell-Mann* by Marco Bersanelli & Mario Gargantini, Templeton Press, 2009
- *Newton's Gift* by David Berlinski, Touchstone, 2000
- *Physics & Philosophy* by Werner Heisenberg, Harper Perennial, 2007

Symmetry (advanced level):

Note: physicists often refer to symmetry (equivalence, sameness, conservation, balance, harmony) as invariance

- *Relativity – The Special & The General Theory* by Albert Einstein, Martino Publishing, 2010
- *Symmetry and the Beautiful Universe by* Leon Lederman and Christopher Hill, Prometheus Books, 2004
- *A Beautiful Question* by Frank Wilczek, Allen Lane, 2015
- *Symmetry – A Journey into the Patterns of Nature* by Marcus du Sauttoy, Harper Perennial, 2009
- *Fearful Symmetry* by A. Zee, Princeton University Press, 2007
- *Deep Down Things* by Bruce. A. Schumm, The John Hopkins University Press, 2004
- *Love & Math* by Edward Frenkel, Basic Books, 2013

Holism & Harmony/Balance with Nature:

- *Drawdown – The Most Comprehensive Plan Ever Proposed To Reverse Global Warming* edited by Paul Hawken, Penguin Books, 2017
- *Harmony – A New Way of Looking at Our World* by HRH The Prince of Wales, HarperCollins*Publishers*, 2010
- *Leonardo da Vinci* by Walter Isaacson, Simon & Schuster, 2017
- *The Invention of Nature* by Andrea Wulf, John Murray, 2015

Epigenetics:

- *The Biology of Belief* by Bruce Lipton, Hay House, 2015
- *Molecules of Emotion* by Candance Pert, Simon & Schuster, 1997

Also by George Hohbach & Ehrengard Hohbach with Scott Marcano: *MICHAEL & MIA*, illustrated Middle Grade Novel

Two young chemistry fans, haunted by a polluting, mad robot, discover a stunning, circular solution in Nature at the last minute that can save their home planet.

A humorous adventure based on the life of C2C co-founder Michael Braungart.

THE C2C MUSIC VIDEO

NATURE LIVES

Song to the
Middle Grade
Novel
Michael & Mia

FULL CYCLES ONLY!